STO

WOMEN IN PRISON

Some twelve thousand women are behind bars in felony prisons all over the country today. In addition thousands of other women are incarcerated in jails and other correctional facilities. Who are these women? Where did they go wrong? What happens to them in prison? What are their chances when they are released? Most of the women are young. Almost none of them ever expected to end up in prison. Some of them find a "home" there.

WOMEN IN PRISON is an eye-opening account of life inside a modern, progressive prison for women. From the moment of her entry as a newcomer or "fish," an inmate is subject to rigid controls. First the institution places restrictions on her. Then she is further controlled by a tightly structured convict society. Privacy and freedom of choice are no longer hers.

Still, many institutions offer some form of rehabilitation, some programs for self-help and education. Most of the women in prison today will eventually be released on parole and returned to society. Will they be ready? Is society prepared to help?

Here is a glimpse into prison life, a penetrating insight into the successes and failures of our penal institutions. WOMEN IN PRISON provides a much-needed consideration of both the problems and the prospects of our penal system.

WOMEN IN
PRISON

EDNA WALKER CHANDLER

THE BOBBS-MERRILL COMPANY, INC.

INDIANAPOLIS   NEW YORK

THE BOBBS-MERRILL COMPANY, INC.

PUBLISHERS   INDIANAPOLIS   NEW YORK

Copyright © 1973 by Edna Walker Chandler
Design by Jack Jaget
Printed in the United States of America
All rights reserved
ISBN 0-672-51702-7
Library of Congress catalog card number: 72-88765
0 9 8 7 6 5 4 3 2 1

To Marcia,
who knows life inside and outside "the gates"
and has made it—outside.

CONTENTS

CONTENTS

FOREWORD

THIS BOOK tells the story of life in a modern, progressive prison for women. I first became aware of the 'prison culture' through a longtime friend who for eleven years was an employee at CIW, California Institution for Women. At her invitation, my husband and I gave a program for the inmates with our African slides and artifacts. We were asked to return with the program the following year. We thus became acquainted with several staff members and a few inmates.

As the writer in our team, I began researching the subject of women's prisons, finding that very little had been published, and that there was nothing at all available for junior high and high school youth. Since this is the age when the delinquency that often leads to crime begins, the idea grew that there was a real need for such a book. But how to get 'inside,' to get the feel of the whole thing? I was not about to commit a crime in order to find out firsthand!

In the meantime, I had become acquainted with Mrs. Iverne R. Carter, then superintendent at CIW, since retired. She also believed that there was need for a factual, objective book that would give an outsider some idea of what it's like to be confined in a modern prison. For whatever the reason a woman is forced to spend time in prison, whether the sentence be short or long, even with the finest opportunities for rehabilitation available, it's still a prison.

In order to gain the 'inside feeling,' I was given the privilege of working as a volunteer teacher on a special permit for three months. During this time I spent two weeks teaching in the institution, then continued (and still do) on a correspondence basis with any student interested in my specialty, creative writing. During that period there were many unscheduled visits with inmates other than my students.

The remainder of my three months was spent interviewing people in the Department of Corrections, staff members at CIW, parolees, directors of halfway houses, and parole agents. All have been most cooperative and helpful. Without such cooperation a book of this kind could not have been written.

The author sincerely hopes not only that this book will be a readable eye-opener to young girls who may be in that very dangerous, shadowy area between delinquency and crime, but that it will help persuade the public to accept more responsibility for the rebuilding of lives.

There are at present thirty-four prisons in the United States designated as places of incarceration for adult women felons. California Institution for Women is one of the largest, and the only one of its kind in California.

The editor at Bobbs-Merrill suggested that we present as much as possible of the women's prison story on a national level. Although originally there had been no intention to go so far afield in the research aspects, a questionnaire was sent to every prison in the country housing adult female felons, prisons which incarcerate women who have been found guilty of such serious crimes against person or property, or both, that they are considered dangerous to society.

The questionnaire was answered by thirty of the thirty-four prisons. Since there was no way to personally visit each institution, the statistics obtained cannot be measured scientifically; however, they do indicate significant trends.

The information gained reveals areas of common weakness in need of public and official attention. The questionnaire also indicates growing awareness of the prison problem at every level. Positive changes have been initiated in many prisons. Others are planned for such a time as funds are made available by state legislation.

The epilogue will give the information obtained from the questionnaire and follow-up correspondence. Nearly all wardens or superintendents have been most cooperative, willing to do everything possible to show the general public what prisons for women are like.

The author does not pretend to sit in judgment on any one institution or state penal system. But it is hoped that making more information available to all will stimulate every state correctional department to take an honest analytical look at its own institutions. Then, as they are supported by a more knowledgeable citizenry, those who have the authority to make progressive changes will do so.

ACKNOWLEDGMENTS

I wish to thank especially the many individuals in the Department of Corrections of the State of California. Without their cooperation this book would have been impossible. All of us who have worked together for so long hope that knowing more of the inside operation of a woman's prison will increase public awareness of the needs of our penal institutions and of what individuals in the free world can and should do to meet those needs.

I wish to thank also all the administrative personnel who were so cooperative in releasing statistical information, and all those who have shared information, opened channels for interviews, and given hours of personal and official time to this project.

While every effort has been made to keep statistical information current, changes already underway in many states make it impossible to present absolutely final and accurate figures.

Last, but definitely not least, thanks also to the women

themselves. I have had the privilege of meeting and counting as friends certain women who won't need to read this book to learn about prison life. They *know*. Many of them are trying very hard to "make it" in the free world. A few find their way quickly. Others slip and fall, not once but often, usually because the obstacles are greater than they are able to overcome at parole time.

I am sincerely grateful for the understanding I have gained by knowing these women.

WOMEN IN PRISON

CHAPTER I

WHATEVER THE NAME, IT'S PRISON

LOCATED between Ontario and Corona, California, an hour from Los Angeles by freeway (if you're free) is a group of buff-colored one-story buildings. The sign at the entrance says CALIFORNIA INSTITUTION FOR WOMEN, *Department of Corrections*. The word *prison* does not appear on the sign; there is no guard tower on the roof. Within these buildings an average of 590 women live, work, attend classes or don't, hate or hope, mark days off the calendar.

Women employees who are expected to keep watch over the residents are called women's correctional supervisors. Male employees who help in custody work are called correctional officers, C.O.'s in prison language. These people may be found at various places inside and out, busy with a variety of duties, but their presence is not emphasized.

Similar places may be called training centers, rehabilitation centers, correctional facilities, institutions, industrial farms, reformatories, or by any other fancy name, but they are still prisons. At the last count in 1971 there were thirty-four prisons under the jurisdiction of the United States that housed adult female felons only. These include the District of Columbia, Puerto Rico, and the Federal Reformatory for Women at Alderson, West Virginia. States which have only a few convicted female felons sometimes contract with another state for their care. This is true for Idaho, Montana, North Dakota and Wyoming. Several states maintain separate buildings adjacent to those housing male prisoners. Florida has programs planned toward meeting the needs of both male and female prisoners in a single facility, with a woman warden heading both divisions. A few states are in the process of changeover to completely segregated institutions for male and female felons. Oregon is one of these.

Of these various institutions the harsh title of *prison* appears in only five states. The remaining states try to soften the designation by using names like those already mentioned, but everyone connected with them is always aware that they are prisons, as evidenced in countless ways.

From the moment a woman convict goes through the gates and hears them close behind her, she knows she is in prison. For the woman in her late teens and early twenties, as many are, this may be the first time in her life that she has actually been forced to stay where she didn't want to stay. She will be there until she has fulfilled the terms of her sentence—'done her stretch,' 'done her time.' Naturally, the inmate whose family has money and will use it to hire a good lawyer carries the vague hope that by some legal maneuvering she can 'beat the rap.' And those whose families either do not care enough or have no money for legal help may still nurse along a faint hope that there will somehow be a chance to escape. But they realize their chances are slim.

Until very recent years there were few convicted women criminals. Society tended to protect women from the conditions that encouraged crime. There were certain things a respectable woman did not do, certain places she did not go. If she became involved in a serious crime, her male partners often took full blame. If her involvement went so far that she was brought to trial, a clever woman, especially an attractive one, could easily influence judge and/or jury to her advantage. If the jury was largely male she was almost sure to get gentle treatment. It was difficult for men to accept the idea that a lovely, frail-appearing, shy little woman could be mixed up in any kind of questionable business, especially violent crime. Perhaps the recent demands by women's organizations for full equality with men is bearing fruit in unexpected ways. Whatever the cause, female involvement in serious crime has increased at an alarming rate during the past ten years. A recent national estimate was a 202 percent increase as compared to a 73 percent increase in crimes committed by men.

Some of this increase has been in felonies. There are many kinds of felony and many differences in state laws about what crimes are to be treated as felonies. The increasing use of drugs in recent years has caused even more differences, more divisions of opinion about what constitutes a felony. In any case, a woman who finds herself in a prison for felons has been in a lot worse trouble than wrecking someone else's car!

For many years no attempt was made to provide separate housing or programs for the woman felon. She was simply a person who had committed a very serious act against the person or property of another, perhaps even to the point of murder. Before the 1930s the female

felons of California were kept in a separate wing or por-
tion of the men's prisons. This was the custom in other
state and federal institutions also, and still is in some.
Often these female convicts were actually 'housekeepers'
for the guards, and their lot in prison too frequently de-
pended on their cooperation with the guards in ways
pleasing to their keepers.

During the early 1900s various women's clubs in California became aware of the situation. But it takes a long
time to bring about changes in social thought. Although
the women's clubs, and many individual women on their
own, worked hard, it was not until 1933 that women
prisoners were moved from San Quentin to Tehachapi.
This was better than the old situation, but there was still
much room for improvement. The move to Corona came
after an earthquake had seriously damaged the Tehachapi
facility. In Corona it became known as the California
Institution for Women, the name it still carries.

California Institution for Women is known as CIW by
the staff, inmates, ex-cons, Department of Corrections,
and others familiar with it. Sometimes inmates and ex-
inmates refer to it as the 'joint.' The letters CIW can be
spoken in a variety of ways, but they are seldom said with
love, for it *is* a prison, and prisons are not known for
their loving-kindness. However, they *can* be instruments
for rebuilding broken lives, for physical and mental self-
improvement, for educational or vocational training
toward a self-supporting goal. Thanks to the efforts of its
second woman superintendent (formerly called a
warden), now retired, CIW is one of the most progressive
of the American prisons for women. While rehabilitation
is a continuing goal under the present administration,
the job is far from completed. All over the United States
we are being forced by circumstances to reexamine our
entire penal system, hoping we can come up with some

better answers for dealing with people in prison. By examining rather closely a woman's prison that is considered more progressive than many others we may learn what things we may be optimistic about, and yet pinpoint other areas that still need attention.

Before getting inside the California Institution for Women, let us consider briefly the reasons why prisons exist. We might call this a look at the evolution of criminal justice as we know it in the United States. Generally speaking, prison administration has advanced from the simple concept of *retribution* (getting even) to holding the individual responsible for *restitution* (restoring or replacing what she has taken or destroyed), to the development of programs for *rehabilitation* of the prisoner. Rehabilitation means changing in a positive way, or rebuilding toward becoming a useful member of society. We will refer to these terms as the three R's of dealing with convicts: retribution, restitution, and rehabilitation.

Our first records of prisons and prisoners reveal attitudes of extreme hatred and vengefulness toward the individual who had broken the law. Certain acts which were once death-penalty crimes today aren't even noticed. For instance, there were the sordid witchcraft trials in Salem, Massachusetts. And thousands of miles away, in Hawaii, people were tossed over the nearest cliff for crossing the shadow of King Kamehameha. Until quite recently, "an eye for an eye, a tooth for a tooth" was the basic idea behind all punishment. As for women, usually they weren't even honored by any kind of trial. Sometimes they were even thrown to the dogs, as was Jezebel of Old Testament times (II Kings, Chapter 9), or maybe stoned for adultery, with their sex partners often the first and most enthusiastic hurlers of the stones. But in general, the punishment was supposed to fit the crime. Guilt did not even need to be proved if public feeling ran high against the accused; he (or she) had killed, or was strongly suspected of being the killer. In turn, he (or she) must be killed, and immediately. This was retribution, the first R of criminal law.

Then came the second R—restitution. A thief was expected to repay what he had stolen. He must either return the actual goods or give back something of equal or greater value. If neither course was possible, he must work, often as a slave, for as many years as were required to make restitution.

Slowly and painfully people's thinking began to change; questioning began in many places, within groups, by individuals.

This national self-examining is still going on, particularly in regard to the death penalty. Now people are asking, does executing a murderer really serve a purpose? The murdered one cannot be restored to life. Still, society must be protected from other killings by the murderer. How can this be assured? Can the punishment actually be made to fit the crime?

Often inmates feel that the first R, *retribution*, or getting even, is the sole aim of the arresting or custodial officer. No one can deny that there *have* been cases of rough treatment. Sometimes this is unavoidable. The prisoner is not sympathetic with the job the officer must do, which is to control the actions of the lawbreaker. On the other hand, a strong, aggressive young female prisoner can make things very difficult for a law enforcement or custodial officer. Often the prisoner either has not learned how to control her own actions or doesn't want to. Sometimes she even brags about how tough she is.

"I didn't get my sentence because of what I *did*, but because of the hell I raised with the cop who took me in. He'll never forget *me*, I'll bet on that!" one attractive young woman was heard to say.

So when a husky young woman violently resists any control, the line between 'necessary control' and 'unnecessarily rough treatment' becomes rather thin.

And what about *restitution:* restoring what was taken, or mending the damage? In cases of embezzlement, forgeries of various kinds, and lesser crimes involving property, perhaps restitution *is* possible and just. But suppose, for example, a person has been kidnapped and held for ransom. The ransom was paid, the victim was released unharmed, the guilty person was caught before the money was spent; every cent was returned. Can any restitution be made for the hours, perhaps days, of fear and agony suffered by the victim and members of his family? So how do we deal with the criminal? He has made restitution, has returned what was taken. But he is still criminal in his attitudes. We wouldn't want him running around loose in the same frame of mind. He might try the same thing again and be more successful next time.

The doubtful outcome of the first and second R's, *retribution* and *restitution,* leads to thinking on the third R: *rehabilitation,* or rebuilding.

At this point California Institution for Women comes into focus again, for it has been active *against* retribution and *for* rehabilitation. This doesn't mean that the administration at CIW or any of the other more progressive prisons is content with the programs underway. Staff would be first to admit, many with real discouragement, that there are weary miles ahead. But the goal is to release women so well prepared for a new, constructive life that they will never again be prison residents. How to do this is the big question.

First, let's examine a few general causes for the rising crime rate of recent years. The 'war babies' of the 1940s are now in their twenties and thirties. The high birth rate of those years is reflected in crime as in any other social

area. Family controls weakened during the fifties and
sixties, resulting in a greater number of violent crimes
committed by very young people. For many years prisons
for women housed inmates whose average age was thirty
to thirty-five. There are still a great number of imprisoned
women in this age bracket, but the number has increased
in the younger groups. CIW reports that 46.5 percent of
the inmates are twenty to twenty-nine years of age. Wardens of other prisons report a noticeable lowering of the
inmates' ages. Add to this the increased use of alcohol,
the alarming use of hard drugs, and the population movement toward big cities, and we have a serious problem.
Compounding that problem are budget cuts for nearly all
institutions dealing with criminals. Several prison wardens have reported plans for definite upgrading of training programs of all kinds within their institutions but
state that these must wait until funds are available.

"Lock 'em up and throw away the key" is one solution
offered. Does anyone know how many new prisons would
have to be built to do this? California's annual cost per
woman felon was $6,820 in 1972. The cost to put that
woman on parole to serve the major part of her sentence
is $600 to $900 per year. If she is under treatment for
narcotics use, the cost is more than the basic $600. The
present trend is to grant parole as soon as legally possible
if the woman is at all ready to cope with the free world.
This raises another big question.

Under the parole system in most states, 95 to 98 percent of all felons now behind bars will one day live among
us. Whether we are looking at a prison for men or one for
women, every new plan to be tried should be weighed
and tested with this fact in mind. Because the average
age of prisoners is much lower than formerly, they will be
living among us for a longer time. But unless the programs inside have changed significantly their attitudes

and thus their behavior, their lives outside will become a 'swinging door' existence—into prison and out again.

Most important of all, the woman felon must *want* to change her life pattern. She must *want* rehabilitation. People sometimes ask, "Does a woman who has gone so deeply into crime that she has been sent to a medium security prison (with maximum security areas within it) really want to rebuild her life? Does she want to change her ways, her attitudes, perhaps even change her residence in order to continue a new life after prison?"

There are no pat answers to that question. Nearly all of them will *say* they want to rebuild their lives, because they know that is the way to impress staff in their favor. Only some of them are sincere. They have realized too late that prison is a place to stay out of, and that crime is what put them there. But when they learn that it's really hard to change attitudes that have been developing for years; that change means steady work on a definite schedule; that it means self-discipline, which they are very short on, they simply give up. A few remain stubbornly and bitterly rebellious from the day of admittance until they go out on parole, if they do.

Some, happily, have the strength to see it through and finally reach the day when they have 'made it' in the free world.

An ex-con, speaking to a group of new parolees, told them what rehabilitation really means. She told it in richly embroidered prison talk which they all understood.

"One thing you gals have to get into your heads is that you're going to have to live a square life, like it or not! If you don't learn that, you'll be right back there in the joint in a month. Whatever your special problem was, stay away from your old buddies. If it was drugs, don't ask a junkie the time of day. Don't even *speak* to him! Nobody is going to stay up nights to see if you come in stoned.

Your P.O. [parole officer] isn't even going to check up on your private life, unless you show signs of going on the lam [violating parole]. Then she might. Your P.O. doesn't want you to go back to the joint. Her job is to keep you out, help you keep straight. But it all comes down to one thing. *You* are the only person who can keep you free. You've got to do it yourself!"

Having 'graduated' from prison, this woman knows the price of rehabilitation. She knows the payments were begun at CIW. She knows they will go on, and *on*, and ON. In this case the woman has 'made it,' and she will continue, for she has that kind of strength. She is realistic, however. She knows there are social forces working against rehabilitation.

There is definite prejudice, often fear, concerning involvement with a woman on parole. A parolee often has trouble getting a job. The community in general ignores her. There are individuals who will actually persecute her, in ways difficult to identify. Often her family too rejects her. And even if they do receive her with open arms, they are not always the type of people who can help her stay 'clean' or 'straight,' in which case she becomes lonely and drifts back to her old associates; she knows they understand her problems. This is the kind of understanding she doesn't need, but often it is all she can get.

Also, she may be very young but with much experience in crime dating back to her early teen years when her crime pattern began to develop. She has seen the inside of youth correctional centers, juvenile homes and reformatories. Then as a young adult she is involved in a very serious crime and is sent to prison as a felon at eighteen, nineteen, or her early twenties. She may be released in a year or so, more rebellious than when she went into prison. Often she has learned a few more 'tricks of the trade,' and feels she is smarter now: she won't get caught next time.

As one former CIW inmate said, "I went into prison knowing just my own thing. You know. What I did to be sent there. I came out with a good education in a lot of other kinds of crime."

When asked how *she* would prevent this kind of happening, she said, "There ought to be closer segregation. If crime has become a way of life for a woman, she feels like a 'big-timer.' She *wants* to tell the greenies all the tricks she knows. Makes her feel like somebody. You know. In prison there isn't a lot you can do to feel important."

What this woman doesn't know is that many prison officials would agree with her but can do little more than they are doing now to segregate according to crime experience. Such changes require money. Getting huge sums of money calls for public awareness and support.

More and more women who are socially aware, financially able and willing, and prepared in their own thinking are accepting the responsibilities of the job of parole advisor. The basic requirement for this role is that the advisor be a 'listener,' the line of communication to help a paroled woman face her own problems. In some cases she may give financial assistance, but she is under no obligation to do so. The most important thing the parole advisor gives is the evidence that there are people in the free world who care what happens to a particular female ex-con.

Some churches and service clubs have definite programs for helping the ex-con return to a positive way of life. But as the first inmate quoted said, it comes right down to the woman herself. Her attitude toward the third R, *rehabilitation,* was formulated in prison.

So what's the story of women in prison? Who are they?

Where do they come from? Why are they in prison? What does it cost to keep them there? Do women prisoners need programs different from those of male convicts? What is a woman's prison really like inside?

Let's take a reader's look at several women 'doing time' in a well-known up-to-date prison for adult women felons. We'll check in with some of them on parole, try to 'feel' with them the forces they must combat in the free world. Perhaps we will begin to understand better and thus be able to deal more wisely with the woman who has been or is now in prison.

But let us keep in mind that California Institution for Women is among four or five very progressive prisons. It is *not* typical of all.

CHAPTER 2

THE GATES

MOST INMATES of an adult correctional institution
have very personal inside knowledge of other such places,
often in several different states. Some were in juvenile
training or correctional centers most of their teen-age
lives. They have been in industrial schools for girls, in
narcotics or alcoholic treatment facilities, mental institutions of various kinds, county jails, and even in federal
prisons.

Usually a woman in California Institution for Women
or one of the other prisons for women felons has been
active in crime for a long time. An inmate who is a first
offender is likely to be a murderess. Those sentenced for
crimes other than first-time murder have reached the
imprisonment point one step at a time. However, in 1971
the picture was a bit different. Twenty-six percent came
to CIW with no prior commitments; that is, without
previous experience in any kind of penal institution.

As with any other group, a prison population has many

kinds of people. Some are highly intelligent, artistic, friendly, easy to talk to, and very much aware of their problems; they accept personal responsibility for being in prison. Others are bitter and hostile toward everyone. Still others are dull, emotionally disturbed, seemingly without motivation toward any method of self-improvement, uncommunicative, and unwilling to accept any blame for their predicament. Between these extremes can be found all the shades of difference.

Fictitious names will be used throughout this book, but these are real women, coming from many kinds of homes or communities. The one thing they all share is the experience of being prisoners. From the first buzzer in the morning to the clang of the automatic door bars at night lockup, their day is planned for them. Every move they make is anticipated or quickly investigated.

What happens to a woman when she first comes to prison? Many different things, depending on the policy routine of the prison, some depending on the woman herself. But certain things happen to all of them, no matter who they are or why they are there.

A new prisoner headed for a term in California Institution for Women goes through two gates. She may be brought in a special prison bus under heavy guard. She herself may be wearing 'cuffs' (handcuffs). She may be seated between a couple of strong custody officers, one of whom will be a woman. They may be quite pleasant in a mechanical sort of way, but they are responsible for delivering this woman prisoner to the next set of officers. They must not for a moment forget their job. If the prisoner is one whose crime has been a particularly terrible one, the watchful manner of those in charge will not be relaxed in any way. This was doubly true if she had received the death sentence before the Supreme Court's 1972 ruling abolishing capital punishment as administered in this country. Prior to this ruling, thirty-three states still had the death penalty for certain capital crimes. At this writing the possibility of reinstating the death penalty through federal legislation is being considered. Because the future status of capital punishment remains uncertain, we will consider only those women who can safely be confined in a medium security prison with maximum security areas within it.

A new prison resident may also be brought to the institution by officers in an official car from the county in which she was tried and convicted. Whether by car or bus, the result is the same. She is no longer mistress of her own coming and going.

The first gate is called the *sally port*. The officer in charge identifies himself and drives forward to the second gate. The same thing happens there. When the second gate shuts, the free world is completely gone.

The car stops at RGC, the reception guidance center. Admission routine begins. If the new prisoner is brought in late at night, and if she is not considered a dangerous person, some of the admission process may be left until the following day. But day or night, certain things must be done.

The 'body receipt' is signed by the lady officer at the RGC desk. This simply states that officer So-and-So delivered Mary B. in safe condition to the officer in charge.

Mary B. was not a dangerous person, just a young woman who had made a lot of mistakes, each more serious than the last. She finally got caught. She had become hooked on drugs and began stealing to support her habit. One thing led to another until here she was, a felon. She had been in many kinds of trouble at different times. When she was fifteen and driving without a license she had been involved in a minor traffic accident. Her father got her out of that. She had been going around with a group of kids who had a lot of fun breaking into schools during weekends. Turning over file cases, throwing ink on the walls, picking up whatever they could sell was real sport. One weekend they got caught, or most of them did. Again Mary B.'s father fixed things, so she got only a small fine and a lecture from the judge.

Soon after that she met Rawley . . . handsome, careless, exciting. What thrills *they* had! Pot parties, a few real good LSD trips, a couple not so good. A time came when she *had* to have stronger stuff; so did Rawley. They pulled off one small filling station burglary, and then one a little bigger, and another bigger yet, and finally armed robbery. Here she was at a women's prison for five to fourteen years. Dad hadn't been able to fix it this time.

Right now she hated everyone. It was really the fault of a bunch of stupid people all the way along. Teachers, cops, jail matrons, Rawley. And she hadn't been quite smart enough. Next time she would be smarter.

The custody officer at RGC doesn't give her much chance to think about anything but this awful present moment.

She is told to remove all her jewelry and to turn over the few personal possessions she has brought. They will be returned to her later, the C.O. says. Everything is listed, and she signs the list. They are taken away in a basket. The small things that made her look a little different and feel a bit special from other women, all were in that basket. She is allowed to keep her watch because it is plain and not very valuable. It wouldn't bring her much in 'bribe goods' or special favors.

If there is any reason at all to believe she may have brought in forbidden articles such as drugs she will have to submit to a body search. Since a growing majority of the new commitments do have a history of serious hard drug use, it is easy to understand why this first search would be a close one. However, if she has come directly from a narcotics treatment center, it will be assumed that she comes in 'clean,' and the body search may be more casual. This is not to say that once inside a drug treatment center or in jail or prison there is absolutely no way to get drugs. Drugs *do* get inside, by various means, in spite of close staff watchfulness. But the penalty for getting caught is so serious that only the most daring or the most hardened addicts will try it.

We will assume that Mary B. came in 'clean,' that she has been free of drugs for some time.

Prisons vary in their commitment procedures but follow a general pattern. If there is nothing to indicate that the new arrival is bringing in forbidden articles, the body search at CIW will take place next day and will actually be a medical examination. When a woman is brought in directly from the street the search will probably be quite thorough, including a vaginal examination. But a prisoner is rarely brought directly 'from the street' unless she is a parole violator or was involved in a crime very near the prison. In the latter case she may be brought directly for temporary confinement. If she comes from a county jail or other correctional center she will have had little or no opportunity to get a knife, a file, a pair of scissors, or a supply of drugs. Women who have obtained such items and are willing to risk the results of a thorough body search can and have been known to conceal some strange things in their body cavities, or in an elaborate hair-do!

Next comes a shower, including a shampoo. Then Mary B. will be given prison-issue clothes and bedding. If her commitment papers show that she has tried to harm herself or others or has been rebellious in a physical manner, she may be given a 'strong dress' and a 'strong blanket.' These are made of material so tough that it can't be torn by hand. A room in RGC will be assigned to her. If she needs special medical or psychiatric treatment she may be in RGC much longer. After her stay in RGC she is assigned to a room (six feet by nine feet) in one of the six cottages. Her room will have a small lavatory, a toilet concealed by a cushion top, a little table for toilet articles, writing paper, pictures, etc. There will be a small closet designed to hang full length only the few clothes she needs. A long, narrow slit in the door to her room will enable a supervisor to look in at any time, day or night: her privacy ended with her commitment to prison.

During the days or weeks in RGC she must go through many more routines. The first is the complete medical examination. At CIW this is quite thorough but dignified and is done by highly skilled doctors and nurses. The new inmate is examined for physical problems which show symptoms, and as well for those which do not. She is checked for venereal disease and for tuberculosis, diabetes, and other chronic illnesses. Careful records are made of drug-use signs such as 'track marks' from prolonged use of an addict's needle. Tattoos, scars, facial problems of various kinds, skin abrasions, and crippling deformities are examined. Entries are made on her record as to whether her physical handicaps are correctable with the facilities available. If they are, great effort is made during her incarceration to remedy or at least improve conditions which may have kept her from becoming an asset to herself, her family, her community.

After the medical examination, she will undergo various other tests. Some will be given by the staff of PTU, the psychiatric treatment unit. The results of these will be used to help determine the need for special treatment or individual counseling and her probable readiness for group therapy.

Then come the educational tests, a whole battery of

them. Most new residents claim to have finished a grade or more of schooling than the records will show. Others may actually have completed the given grade but in a very haphazard way, or so long ago that most of what they learned has been lost; thus, they tend to test out lower than the grade level claimed.

Inmates counter this by saying that the tests are given too soon after commitment. They feel they do poorly because they are too scared, sick, upset or confused. However, records on follow-up testing seem to bear out the idea that even those first tests give a fairly accurate picture of a woman's educational level (based chiefly on reading ability), her strong points and her weak ones. Only in the case of a woman who has recently had drugs, liquor, or a particularly severe emotional shock will the first testing be questioned. It will definitely be questioned if the scores are much lower than her general behavior indicates they should be. If it is quite evident that the new resident is not in condition for them, the tests will be postponed until she gains some measure of emotional steadiness. During this period it may become apparent that she cannot respond at all to educational testing. Instead, she may need very close supervision and frequent counseling.

When the test records are placed on file, the new inmate is assigned to a counselor. How much time the counselor will be able to spend with each resident depends on her case load. Alabama reports case loads as high as 126. Only the smaller prisons appear to have comparatively light case loads. However, three states, Delaware, Nebraska and West Virginia, have no professional counselors. Delaware calls in counseling help only when it is needed. Iowa uses a team staff system with counseling as part of the job. A case load of 60 appears to be about average. However, because some states did not answer this item on our questionnaire, our picture is not complete.

The relationship between prisoner and counselor should be the most helpful staff contact of all. There are many instances at CIW and other such places where a counselor has been a constant upward guide and understanding support of a woman's smallest effort to improve her situation. Although the case load of 120 per counselor at CIW is considered fair—that is, not an overload—it is obvious that, as in the case of schools and other guidance centers, the counselor will usually be seeing only the most difficult cases. The quiet, tied-in-knots woman who may need counseling desperately may get little attention, yet she may be the one who needs it most. Or because she *is* shy and tied in knots she may not respond quickly to counseling. She may need more time to get unwound, and counselors don't always have that kind of time. Sometimes they too reach the end of their resources.

Through counseling sessions an inmate is helped to choose an educational goal or some field of vocational training that will prepare her to be self-supporting when she is released. This is particularly important when she has children she must plan to support.

There are cases in which, although the counselor and others involved try every approach that shows the slightest promise, the new prisoner remains hostile. No matter what is suggested, she refuses to be motivated toward any kind of constructive or learning program. California's indeterminate sentence provides an excuse for some women to do nothing to change their life pattern or attitudes. The counselor tries very hard to change this point of view.

Mary B. sits in front of the counselor's desk. She has listened to the results of her tests and to what the counselor thinks that she, Mary B., can and should do to improve her prospects for the future.

"You're a very intelligent young woman, Mary," the counselor says. "You were one of the best 'paper hangers' [check forgers] the court had ever tried, and the slickest young burglar, if that's anything to be proud of. With a brain like that you can do anything you want to do. Your record shows you quit school the middle of your junior year. That's pretty sad. But you can still finish, and you should."

Mary B. stirs enough to answer.

"How do I know I'll be here long enough to finish school? Anyway, I'm pregnant. Gotta take time out to take care of that business. No use to start something I can't finish. Like you said, I've done too much of that already."

"You've twisted my words into something I didn't mean at all," the counselor says. "Things aren't *that* hopeless. You've been no trouble in here so far. Keep on playing it cool and you'll probably only serve your minimum time, and that's . . ." she turns a page, looking for the court record.

"Twenty months," Mary B. finishes the sentence. "School just isn't for me, even if my minimum time is just twenty months. I'll probably get maximum. That's the way my luck goes. I'll be an old woman by then and nothing's going to matter."

As in any other areas of work, counselors are human beings, too. Some are excellent, well-trained, with a real gift for dealing with people. A few, however, view their jobs only as a way to make a living; many have serious personal problems themselves. Most counselors in the larger prisons for women know what should be done and try hard to do it.

Mary B. has difficulty responding to *any* counselor. Now she settles back into a blob of indifference, hearing only those words 'minimum time.' Every time they are spoken it is like being on the receiving end of a club, and the club gets heavier and heavier. Still unable to face the reality of her situation or her own responsibility for it, she retreats from the scene as completely as she can.

"O.K." the counselor says, "we'll assign you to a group. You'll meet with Group X in the audio room Wednesday after lunch. Maybe you'll find some women there who are worse off than you are!"

The counselor makes notes on Mary B.'s schedule sheet. "So long, Mary. I'll see you again in a couple of weeks."

Mary B. mutters something that sounds vaguely like a curse. She slouches from the room, taking along her schedule sheet with complete absence of enthusiasm.

The counselor makes an entry on Mary B.'s case history: "Subject Mary B. very unresponsive to any suggestions for positive action. Have assigned her to Wednesday's group but have doubts that she is ready yet for grouping. She may never be."

Mary B. goes to her assigned room in one of the cottages. This will be her room for her entire stay unless for some serious reason she is placed elsewhere. She has been given sheets which give the rules of the place, the commissary hours, visiting privileges, and regulations on what can be sent to her by her family or friends and what items are forbidden. From this day on for as long as she is in prison she must live within the bounds set forth by the prison rules.

Mary B. is now a 'fish,' a newcomer to prison, ready to be tried out by her fellow inmates. She will be assigned a job and caught up in the routine of the institution. She will be rebellious and hostile, submissive and docile, as the mood suits her. As her body grows heavy with her advancing pregnancy, her steps will be even slower, more plodding. She will be 'doing her time' and nothing else.

Mary B. may never be ready for grouping or for any other improvement program in any prison. Successful rehabilitation is a real problem for the Mary B. people, either in or out of a correctional institution.

CHAPTER 3

THE 'FISH'

Just WHY a newly committed prisoner should be called a 'fish' is something no one seems to be able to explain. But the word is well understood in both men's and women's prisons, in jails, and in the various correctional training centers.

Actually, there are few women in the California Institution for Women who can be considered 'fish' in the sense of being new to crime. A woman felon has usually walked progressively down a long, hard road, her trail marked by legal scoldings and periods of probation for minor misdemeanors. These were followed by a series of petty crimes each more serious than the last, until finally she is involved in a felony. So, as crime knowledge goes, CIW residents are not innocent children. As one inmate stated, "Sure, we're guilty of some kind of law-breaking, every one of us. We may not be guilty as charged, but we're not here for going to Sunday school!"

But as their experience in CIW goes they are 'fish,'

newcomers, untried, unknown by other inmates. Sometimes a woman knows in advance that a friend is there
or soon learns that she is. Usually the new resident sees
her fellow prisoners as a sea of blank faces at mealtime,
as unknown as staff. All she has in common with them is
that she too is in a felons' prison, lonely, her liberty lost,
her rights gone. She has little sense of personal worth;
perhaps in addition she is eaten with bitterness and sub-
dued hostility.

She will soon learn that the inmate code is already
in motion, set to find out where she stands on various
things. Exceptions to this are the women under sentence
of death. They are the untouchables, confined in the
maximum security unit under constant guard. They have
no contact with the remainder of the prison population.
But the other prisoners have a social structure as hard
to crack as that of any exclusive club on the outside.
Its members want to fit the 'fish' into the structure, to
find out her possible usefulness for getting favors or
contraband. But she will be put through many tests before
she is accepted.

First, how does she stand on 'snitching,' the greatest
inmate crime of all? If she shows signs that she is a
snitcher or could become one, leave her alone! The word
gets around that she will line up with staff. She can never
be trusted with inside information. She will be con-
demned to walk her own road, every step of it alone.
Just how will she be tested? It can happen in many different ways. A frequent testing place is in the first meal
lineup.

The line begins to form at 5:00 P.M. and by 6:00 the
serving begins. Most of the women look forward to the
dinner hour, for the meals are usually good and it's a
time for a bit of socializing. CIW allows considerable
flexibility at dinner hour. The women sit at tables with

their special friends in groups of four to six. Woe to the woman who tries to barge in on one of these tight little gatherings! If she is invited to come in, that's something else.

"Look a'comin'!" Jo said in a low, muffled voice. "New, and scared as all hell. A real 'fish.'"

"Ask her to eat with us," a woman nearby suggested. "We got an empty place since Kath went out."

Eyebrows flicked in knowing ways, saying 'yes' in their own silent language.

Jo turned, got eye contact with the stranger. Smiling in invitation, she put across the idea of welcome.

The newcomer smiled, nodded. The woman next to Jo said, "I'll trade places with her." There was great respect in her voice as she spoke to Jo.

She had reason to respect Jo, the most important 'butch' in the whole prison. Jo's mannish looks, low-slung belt and masculine-style vest told only part of the story. The rest was in her strong, well-built body, her iron-muscled arms that could beat with a towel-wrapped bar of soap until her victim was unconscious, with never a bruise on her entire body.

As an attractive, high-grade butch she could have any 'turned-out' woman she wanted as her homosexual partner. Many of the women in CIW had a real and personal knowledge of Jo's various qualities. Now she was about to pave the way for trying out another 'fish' as she had tried out dozens of others.

Frightened, younger than most and prettier than the average, this one should put on a good show, a bit of diversion for the evening.

"Hi, baby!" Jo greeted as the new woman took the place offered. "What do we call you?"

"Mary."

"That's good. Haven't had a Mary in here for a long time."

Jo introduced others in the group without mentioning the reason for their being there. Nor did she ask Mary what had brought her to this place. That would be up to Mary to tell or not to tell.

With a plodding kind of shuffle the women went along, finally stopping in front of the serving tables. Jo sniffed, looked over the food in the steam table.

"H'm, fair to middlin' . . . mushroom soup, stuffed peppers, black-eyed peas, okra, pineapple salad. Give my friend here a nice big helping of everything," Jo ordered the woman with the serving spoons. "She's new here, been through a lot lately. You know how it is . . ."

"Please, I—I don't want any black-eyed peas," Mary protested as the big spoon came up with its maximum load.

"Sure you do! You'll change your mind when you get to the table. It's pretty good here as joint food goes. Now some of the places I've been they give you slop—and I mean *slop!*"

Mary accepted the black-eyed peas, knowing she wouldn't eat them.

"Tea, coffee, or milk?" asked the one who served the drinks.

"Tea, but no sugar," Mary answered.

"Sure she wants sugar. Two lumps," Jo interrupted.

The testing was in full swing. Mary allowed the sugar to be placed on her tray, feeling completely conquered by the tall woman with the deep voice.

At the table Jo was in command. "You still don't want those black-eyed peas?"

"I don't want them," Mary answered in a precise little voice.

"Well, give 'em to Sally here. She's up from Alabama. Down there they wean kids on black-eyed pea soup."

The women laughed as Jo scraped the peas onto Sally's tray, returned Mary's tray.

"Change your mind about the sugar?" she asked.

"No, take it," Mary answered. Jo's long fingers reached out, but Mary didn't see her touch the sugar cubes. Next thing she knew there was a little pile of cubes beside Jo's plate. Suddenly they disappeared.

"Jo here can boost anything she wants," one woman said admiringly.

"Why not?" Jo asked, her voice amused but scornful. "I'm lookin' ahead. That's what we're told to do here. Look ahead, plan, set a goal. All that stuff. Well, I got a goal. Plenty of hootch for Christmas!"

Appreciative laughing tinkled around the table.

Jo looked into Mary's face, searching, trying out. "You wanta learn to boost?" she asked.

"Maybe."

"No maybes. You do or you don't!" A tense silence settled over the table. Eating tools clicked, but no word was spoken.

Mary broke the silence. "O.K., I want to learn to boost. Anything you want to teach me, I want to learn!"

"Good goin'!" Jo answered softly. "You're O.K. You're gonna be my people. You hear now?" Her glance at the others dared them to protest. No one did.

Mary, the 'fish,' had made her choice. She had been received into the inmate social structure, at least into the outer fringes of it. She was committed.

But the testing had only begun.

A transistor radio disappeared. A shake-down was ordered, and the radio was found in Mary's room. She was almost sure who had put it there, but she said nothing in her own defense. Ten days in 'rack' (isolation) was a small price to pay for acceptance and protection. She had proved she was no snitch.

The homosexual trial was yet to come.

Shortly after she was out of 'rack' Jo came to her as she was busy in the yard.

"You're a doll," Jo said. "You're my people. You know?" She smiled knowingly and put her hands on Mary's breasts caressingly. Her touch was warm, affectionate.

"You turned on, honey?" she asked.

"No—never tried it with a woman, that is."

"I could turn you on. I'm good at it! In here it's the best we got, you know. No kids gonna come from it, either."

Mary shook her head, afraid to say no but determined not to say yes.

"I'm married," she answered, hoping the lie would excuse her.

"So are most of the broads in here. Or have been one time or another. That don't matter."

Still Mary shook her head. "You've been good to me, Jo, and if I could be a femme for anybody it would be for you. But I can't. You see I love that guy I'm married to. He's waiting out there for me [another lie; Rawley wouldn't wait for any woman]. If I let you have me I'd be thinking of him all the time, and it just wouldn't be any good. Not for you—not for me."

It was the most talking Mary had done since she'd been there, and she was scared. No one said no to Jo on anything! And now she, Mary, a fish, had dared to say it. She looked across the campus to the nearest place where a staff member would be stationed, a place of safety. It was too far away! Desperately swallowing the lump of fear in her throat, she turned to her butch friend.

"I'll tell you what. I won't let any other broad have me. When I've been here a long time I may change my mind. If I do, I'll let you know. O.K.?"

Lovingly she laid her head against Jo's shoulder. Jo

hugged her, kissing her affectionately, without passion. The crisis had passed.

Both women heard footsteps on the walk around the building corner. Quickly they separated, stepping apart. Mary became very busy with her yard work.

"What are you doing here, Jo?" the yard supervisor asked. "This isn't your work assignment."

"I just stopped to speak to Mary," Jo answered. "Can't even speak to a friend in this place without gettin' the third degree for it. I was on my way to clean the gym and I wanted to say hi! That's all."

"Well, get along then." Turning to Mary, the supervisor said, "Don't play around with that woman. She's no good for anybody, especially not for a fish like you!"

Jo cursed softly, but the work supervisor either didn't hear or chose to ignore her. Jo walked away, her face a sullen mask, her hips twisting in the most sensual way she could manage.

There are many opinions about homosexuality, inside prison and out. It's even difficult to get agreement on when certain behavior becomes homosexual. To some staff, any physical contact (P.C., personal contact), such as holding hands, arms around the waist, hugging, or the lightest kissing is suspect and should be stopped, or at least discouraged. Others draw the line at actual sexual play. Still others ignore even that in the belief that sometimes sexual contact between consenting adults of the same sex may relieve tensions that otherwise could lead to more dangerous activities.

Studies have shown that the real danger of homosexual relationships in the prison situation lies in the fact that violent jealousies may develop. Women have been known to beat other women to unconsciousness, leaving them scratched and mutilated, all in a battle for the sexual favors of an especially desirable woman (femme).

Also, if one partner goes out on parole before the other, she may return to her husband or other male partner. When her prison partner is released and tries to renew the old attachment, the heterosexual woman is in trouble.

No one denies that homosexual couples are numerous in prison. Any situation regarded as a social problem outside has a counterpart in prison. Such close confinement tends to intensify relationships which in the free world might be only incidental. There is too often little else of a warm, human, personal contact in prison except a homosexual one.

It is impossible to give any meaningful figures on the extent of homosexuality because of lack of agreement on what is and what is not. One woman said she believed that about 90 percent of the women had at some time had homosexual experience.

"Some were 'gay' before they came," she said. "They went to 'gay bars,' hung out with the gay crowd. They're not about to change in here. The others?" She shrugged. "Well, you just sometimes get hungry to feel another human body real close, see if it's warm, if *you're* warm— if you're alive yet. If that's a sign of being homo I guess all of us are to some extent."

And the testing of the 'fish' continues. If she stays to herself and doesn't snitch, but will take no part in rule-breaking escapades, she's left alone. She is not considered trustworthy in big things like a planned escape, so she's never taken into the 'inner courts.' She holds an attitude of "You do your time, I'll do mine." Sometimes this is her verbal answer to anyone who asks her questions about touchy happenings.

A few become personally involved with staff in one way or another. Sometimes other inmates 'use' such

women to get special privileges, more commissary opportunities and so on. Those in staff confidence can
feather their nests well by exchanging information for
cigarettes, for cosmetics, even for drugs in some cases.
Although staff may not knowingly reveal any inside information, inmates who work in offices, handle files, or
have access to rooms where they may accidentally come
upon valuable bits of news are in positions that are
potentially either dangerous or advantageous to them.
Highly intelligent women often do push their luck as far
as possible, gaining for themselves certain 'salable' items.
There's nothing quite like the tightrope-walking found
within a prison society!

Whatever slot she settles into in the prison social
structure is largely up to the new 'fish.' When she has
found it she will be expected to live up to it through every
grinding day inside. If she snitches even once, the word
will go with her; if she has a good line to the 'straights,'
that too will be remembered and used whenever possible.
Whatever her slot image she will never be allowed to
step out of it for one moment, not even if she becomes a
leader herself, a recognized tester of other 'fish.' It will
go with her as a long shadow through her confinement,
her entire parole period, sometimes all the rest of her
life.

CHAPTER 4

THE NITTY-GRITTY OF PRISON LIFE

Aᴌᴛʜᴏᴜɢʜ most of the women in a state prison have had previous experience in some kind of correctional institution, they know that each place has its own routine, its own regulations. In some places these regulations are very confining, almost inflexible; in others they are less so. In all cases the flexibility depends largely upon the philosophy of the administrative staff. If the warden, director, superintendent—whatever name she is called— believes that a felons' prison exists almost entirely to protect society from dangerous people and to punish the transgressor, the regulations will tend to be strict and slow to change.

If, on the other hand, those in charge see the prison residents as people who have made serious mistakes but who for the most part can be retrained in a self-supporting vocation, whose attitudes can be changed to the point where they may safely return to the outside world as contributive members of it, then the policies will tend to

33

be less restrictive and more readily changed. Such administrators will not lose sight of the fact that some of the imprisoned women *are* dangerous criminals, that they have committed such offenses as armed robbery and assault with a deadly weapon. Some have killed— and would not hesitate to kill again. However, it is generally accepted by those who have made a study of prisons that a relatively small percentage will fit into this category: some put it at 5 percent; others say it may be as high as 8 to 10 percent. This small but dangerous percentage must be kept in a carefully managed and controlled environment, a few in strict custody. In some cases even their inmate associates are afraid of them. As one resident said of another, "I'm scared to death of So-and-So. If she told me to help her get a rope for a try at escape, I'd be stupid not to do it. She'd choke me to death if I didn't. So I stay out of her way. I don't even walk across campus with her unless it's broad daylight."

For both safety and efficiency, the prison area must be organized to meet the needs of many different kinds of people.

During the period of RGC (reception guidance center) a new inmate is confined in medium security unless she brings a history of violent behavior, in which case she will be held in a maximum security room until she is able to discipline herself to life in medium security.

Maximum security also includes those under death sentence. Such security may be temporarily imposed on those women who are emotionally so disturbed as to be dangerous to themselves or others. Temporary maximum security is also used to punish rule-breaking. At CIW the limit is ten days in 'rack,' as the women call this kind of confinement.

Prior to the current inward look that is being taken at all penal systems in the U.S., there was a tendency at some prisons to put a rebel in 'rack' or isolation to get her out of the way. Sometimes she was kept for such an indefinite time that her existence was almost forgotten.

This method of dealing with the rebel is changing in the progressive prisons, rapidly in some, very slowly in others. People in charge are seriously asking how to make a short period in isolation a positive treatment rather than a negative, purely punitive one. Most of us in the free world would become very hostile if we were locked in a small room with barred windows so high that nothing was seen of the outside except light; if we saw no one except the cottage supervisor or custody officer; if we were completely cut off from even the social contacts of prison life, with nothing to do except read one of the few books available. If a woman's educational level is so low that she can't even read well enough to enjoy adult material, she has nothing to fill her time except to eat when food is brought, take a shower when the supervisor is there, use the toilet—and generate hostility. How can she be other than hostile after her term in 'rack'?

This is not to say it is never necessary to punish serious rule-breakers. The woman is in prison in the first place because she broke one or more of the rules or laws of the social structure. One of the lessons she needs to learn in prison is to control her own actions so that she will become a law-abiding citizen, not a lawbreaking one. If she considers the laws she has broken to be bad or unjust, she must learn that there are constructive ways to change them. Meanwhile, perhaps better programs can be devised for women in maximum security for whatever time they spend there.

The next degree of confinement is called close custody, not quite so rough as maximum security but almost. The inmate must be accompanied by a custody officer at all times. She takes meals in the dining room, goes to group sessions, for counseling, to the hospital if necessary, but always in the company of a custody officer. Night activities are usually closed to her.

Medium security is the overall type of confinement under which most prisons for women are organized. Other degrees of security branch out from the medium security standard, either more or less strict. A medium security resident may participate in any activity available to her within the limits of the institution. She has considerably more freedom than those in stricter confinement, but she is still very limited. After all, this *is* prison, and she is reminded of it every hour of her day and night.

The most desirable kind of confinement inside a prison is minimum security. This category allows freedom for any activity within the general schedule and rules. Classes in school, work assignments, attendance at night activities, commissary buying, all these are open to the woman on minimum security. She may even stay up to see the late movie on TV.

If she proves able to live within minimum security, she may soon be allowed other privileges, such as work furlough, 72-hour passes, and family visitation.

One of the first things a new resident wants to know is just where the lines will be drawn in this particular prison. Are they quite strict? More flexible? Which staff members are 'hard,' quick to see the smallest move toward breaking a rule, quick to accuse without much thought? Are there staff members who might look the other way, especially on rules that do not threaten the security of either residents or staff? In most cases other residents will give their opinion if asked and if they think they can trust the newcomer not to 'snitch.' But in general the new resident must find out for herself, make her own judgments.

All prisons have rule lists that are either given out

individually or posted in cottages, dining rooms or other places of gathering. Every inmate is held responsible for learning and keeping in mind the regulations she must observe. First she will be given sheets, pillowcase, and spread for her room. She will be told when she is to send bedding and personal things to the laundry. She will be given certain times for doing her own personal laundry. She will be assigned an institutional job to which she must report at a stated time. Some of these jobs, such as breakfast detail, begin very early. This may be a hard job to do, especially if she had a problem adhering to a job or school schedule in her pre-prison days. Here she has no choice. She will learn to listen for and respond to the various sounds of routine—the automatic bar sliding across her door at count time, sliding back at wake-up time; the buzzer or bells for reporting to classes or work; the click of the intercom (if there is one) as a voice comes on to give a general announcement.

There will be regular hours for meals, and in a large prison there may be "first and second lines." Early birds go to the first lines; the first food served is the most tasty. But some don't value that as an incentive, they go to second line. If they have some kind of emotional problem, perhaps they don't go at all. If refusal to eat continues, the counselor investigates. The woman may be ill, may need hospitalization or psychiatric help at once. Many prisons are severely criticized for the type and quality of food served the inmates and in some cases this criticism is deserved. In CIW it is not. Even inmates who have been elsewhere admit that the food at CIW is good, "if anything in prison can be good." For some it is much better than the meals they had before prison, and they know that here they will, or at least can, have three good meals every day. But it's still institutional food, cooked in enormous quantities, which in itself lowers the quality

no matter what the cook does to upgrade it. And it's eaten
in the company of scores of other people, all here because
of serious problems of one kind or another. (The table-
talk is not likely to be very inspiring!) In a modern, progressive women's prison, these may well be the dinner
menus for the week:

Monday
Chilled Juice
Stuffed Peppers & Rice
Carrot & Pineapple Salad
Hot Roll & Butter

Tuesday
Clam Chowder
Fish Platter, etc.

Wednesday
Chicken, Steak, Pork Chop
  or Cutlet

Thursday
Tomato Soup
Braised Ribs   Potatoes
Broccoli   Peach Salad

Friday
Pineapple Juice
Baked Ham
Potato Salad
Green Beans
Cole Slaw

Saturday
Tomato Juice
Mexican Plate
Tostado Relleno
Beans & Rice

Sunday
Vegetable Soup
Roast Beef   Cream-Style Corn
Cabbage Lime Salad

Other meals are of similar high quality.

Besides eating, sleeping, going to a job or going to
school, there are other routines to learn. The pill line,
for instance. At 4:00 P.M. all women on medication go
to the hospital to receive their medicine. There they
wait in a long line, some obviously not well, others looking so healthy that one wonders why they are there. The
nurse or nurse's aid comes down the line with her pills
and cups of water. She stands there until the woman
swallows the pill. There is a reason for this. Some pills are
powerful tranquilizers; they must be taken as directed.
If they are hoarded and taken for other reasons they can
produce a 'high,' or a 'low,' or even be lethal. So, although

it may be only aspirin, the nurse must see that that pill goes where it was intended to go.

Then there's the business of sending and receiving letters and packages, so familiar to free people that we don't even think of it as a privilege.

Most prisons have some kind of mail control, but the more progressive have what is known as open correspondence. This means an inmate may correspond with anyone on her approved contact list. An inmate who wishes to correspond with an inmate of another institution must have approval of the administration. In open correspondence an inmate may also receive and send as many letters as she wishes. CIW is one of those prisons for women having open correspondence. But, as in most prisons, all mail is subject to inspection; it may or may not be censored. It's hard to write freely to anyone, knowing that the letter may be read. Some states have a policy of 'liberal censorship.' Others admit their censorship is close.

Packages brought to CIW by visitors must be properly wrapped, with the name of the sender and the name of the inmate for whom the package is intended on the outside of the package. Form CIW 203 APPROVAL OF INCOMING PACKAGES must be attached or enclosed in the package. All packages coming in or going out by mail are checked in the mailroom. Form CIW 203, approved by the mailroom supervisor, *must* be enclosed.

Women who have the funds are able to order items of personal property from Sears Roebuck through the CIW Canteen. The types and quantities are governed by the same limitations that apply to personal items sent in from home.

Most prisons have a small store so that inmates can buy personal items such as toothpaste, cosmetics, writing paper and cigarettes, small luxuries such as candy and cookies. At CIW these items carry a price tag higher than the same item would cost outside. The extra money goes to the Inmate Welfare Fund. This money at CIW has been used to buy a TV, a stereo and records, and other things that all may enjoy.

Although all inmates except those in maximum security may purchase from the store or commissary, they must follow certain regulations for doing so. They may draw money from their account, but only at certain times. This is done according to their institution number. The 'first draw' women get first choice of items available; 'second draw' get second choice, etc. While this can be a source of tension if items are scarce, it seems to work fairly well. However, the point is that this is another kind of control to which a prison resident must bow.

During the first few days or even weeks in prison, the new resident feels terribly cut off from all she has known. Losses of personal privacy such as unannounced room searches (shake-downs) or eyes peering at her through a slot in the door at count times are a painful shock. She is in a vacuum, a non-society, separated from family and friends and not yet a part of her new social environment. Will she see her family again? If so, when and under what conditions?

In every prison in the country there are persons who have no family. No one will come to see them. Or worse, perhaps the family has completely rejected them and want no further contact with the prisoner. "She made her bed. Let her lie on it!" Their only hope for outside contact is with their religious advisor (if they have one), their lawyer—which isn't likely if the family is disinterested— or a volunteer worker who will act as a 'listener,' in some cases a teacher. These must be people who can be trusted not to bring in contraband, not to resist search if it is considered necessary, not to incite to riot—in fact, people whose motive is strictly a desire to help other human beings.

Luckier are the hundreds of prisoners who do have families who care enough to visit. Sometimes the families live far away. As one woman said, "No one in my family is going to come a thousand miles to see me. They can't afford it, for one thing." But often the family lives near enough to visit. There is a visitation policy of some kind in operation at all prisons. What that policy is depends somewhat on the attitudes of the members of the state penal system, but more especially on the administration in direct charge of each institution.

Visiting policies range from the very restrictive, where the inmate visits through a screen with a custodial officer in the background, to family and/or conjugal visiting, with many shades of difference between these extremes. A schedule must be adhered to. One's parents, children, husband, or good friend doesn't just 'drop in.' The visitor must be approved and must come at certain designated hours. The general visiting regulations at CIW are:

Any person on a woman's approved visiting list may visit her twice a month. Visiting on weekdays will not be limited to a specific length of time. On weekends, visiting will be limited to one hour for local visitors. For those visitors traveling over 100 miles, visiting will be unlimited according to available space.

Children of residents may visit on any visiting day as often as possible. Children of approved visitors must be accompanied by an adult on the approved visiting list.

No visitor will be permitted to visit more than one inmate unless that visitor is a member of the immediate family of more than one.

Visitors falling into the following categories may visit *only* with the approval of the superintendent or delegated staff:

    a. Ex-prisoners of any state or federal facility.
    b. Anyone currently on parole or probation.
    c. Any ex-CIW staff member.
    d. Any person involved with and/or convicted
       of any type of narcotics offense.

Anyone who is barefoot or who is wearing any extreme dress will not be permitted to visit.

Anyone found bringing any items of contraband into the institution will lose his mail and visiting privileges.

VISITING SCHEDULE

CIW AND RGC

Monday	NO VISITING
Tuesday through Friday	9 A.M. to 11:30 A.M.
	1 P.M. to 4 P.M.
Saturday and Sunday	9 A.M. to 4 P.M.

There will be no visiting on weekdays between the hours of 11:30 A.M. and 1 P.M.

In addition, special days are set up for children to visit. Great preparation is made for these days, and both staff and residents feel that such occasions do much to strengthen family ties. They help to prepare the family to accept the mother when she returns to them, and they keep before the mother the fact that she still has these children, and that she will be expected to take care of them when she is released.

More and more state prison systems are planning ahead for construction of cottage or apartment facilities that will provide a more normal family environment. This would mean conjugal visits for married inmates and for those living in recognized common-law marriages.

All prisons allow close kin, religious guides, and other approved persons to see a prisoner if the prisoner so requests. But only CIW has the family visitation plan in the broader, more private sense. This was begun during the summer of 1971. Residents heartily approve this big change and feel it is definitely a step up toward the third R, rehabilitation. Under the plan a woman may have her family for a forty-eight-hour visit if:

1. She is within six months of parole consideration.
2. She is in minimum custody.
3. She has a clear conduct record (no write-ups for six months).

A policy became effective in March 1972 that allowed eligible long-termers to have family visits six months after entering the institution.

During the visit the inmate is allowed the use of a three-room apartment plus bath. This gives the family a living room, bedroom and kitchenette. Cooking equipment, dishes, and linens are furnished. The family brings in food supplies.

The inmate must remain on the grounds of the institution, reporting at the reception desk four times a day, 8:00 A.M., 12:00 noon, 6:00 P.M., and 10:00 P.M. This takes a lot of time from the precious forty-eight hours, but the women accept it as a necessary restriction.

It is generally accepted that a woman cannot be completely separated from her family without great and sometimes irremediable personal damage.

Those who have had a forty-eight-hour visiting experience feel it's a great step toward renewing family ties. Also it reminds them that family life, loving and warm as it may be, brings with it certain problems which the woman must learn to face again. Away from it so long, in her memory she tends to glorify what she has left, forgetting many of the pressures of day-to-day living, housekeeping and mothering. This extended visit with her family reminds her that she must renew her strength in that area.

A majority of the women in prison have small children,

an average of two-plus each. For 500 women this means
that more than a thousand minor children are around
somewhere, without their mothers. They may be with
relatives, in foster homes, or, sad to say, themselves in
correctional institutions.

In addition, many women come to prison pregnant.
Their babies will be born in the prison hospital or clinic
if there is one; if not, the mother-to-be is cared for at an
outside medical facility. During 1972 there were 227
babies born to women in the thirty prisons reporting.

Institutions vary in their handling of this problem. At
CIW twenty-five babies were born in the prison hospital
in 1972. The mothers were allowed to keep them for ten
days. Then the babies were taken to relatives or to foster
homes or released for adoption.

A woman newly committed to prison has sharp, tor-
turing memories of her family. Her feelings of personal
guilt are very deep as she faces the realities of a long
separation from her children. Most of the inmates do
have children, some very young. The fact that many were
very poor mothers only adds to their self-guilt. Good
resolutions are common among prison-bound mothers.
They often run like this:

"If I ever get out of here, I'm going to take my kids and
cut out, start all over. They deserve a lot better break than
I've given them."

As the days and weeks wear on, good resolutions
weaken. The mental images of children or whatever
family unit there is tend to fade. For when the family
lives far away, as is often the case, the mother has only
letter contact. Her older children write less and less often,
and finally not at all. The shame of having a mother in
prison is no help to a teen-ager who has serious problems
of his own.

Women sometimes deliberately allow the ties with the

older children to break down—for the child's good, they say. "What my kid doesn't need is an ex-con mom around his neck. I'm not even going to contact him when I get parole." Whether this kind of resolve will hold is doubtful in many cases. The fact of motherhood is difficult to forget. There is a great desire to see the child, and it grows as the possibility becomes real. "What does he [she] look like now? Is he doing well in school, or did he cop out like his mom did? Maybe I don't want to know . . ."

This, then, is the nitty-gritty, the everyday reality of life in prison. It will vary from one institution to another, but one factor is common to all. Prison routine is of necessity restrictive. Although certain restrictions are necessary, they are in themselves self-defeating, for they further decrease an individual's ability to make desirable personal plans and hold to them. The basic needs of survival—food, clothing, and shelter—are supplied at state expense. But the opportunity to *choose* one's food, clothing, shelter, and companions is gone. The freedom to have any more than free board and room on the taxpayers' credit card was wiped out when the gates clanged shut behind the newly committed resident.

Where and how to draw the line between restrictions that are necessary for safety and efficient management and restrictions used as a means of punishment or retribution is the big question today. People inside prison, both staff and inmates, have been asking this question for a long time. Those of us on the outside, free to manage our own lives, have only just begun to ask. Perhaps we need to seek more diligently for better answers.

CHAPTER 5

SCHOOL DAYS IN PRISON

IT WAS the first Monday of the second semester of school.

Anita J. sloshed a mop across a small area of the huge dining room floor. She worked near the windows so she could see the women going toward the school. The after-breakfast cleanup was easier than the after-dinner cleaning, so there was more time to watch the activity outside the windows. Between mop pushes that were far from enthusiastic she watched the women making their way to the school building back of the gym.

Their faces told different stories. On some the dull, flat lines of resignation were all too plain. A few were openly hostile and rebellious. On others there was a look of hope, almost happy anticipation. Some women carried books, chatted with friends, greeted teachers also headed for classrooms.

These were the women who had decided to return to school. Anita J. wouldn't admit even to herself that the women she watched were taking a very important step toward a better life in the free, outside world. Anita J. was one of those who refused to accept any program as something that would help her.

Anita had been so good with figures that she became an embezzler. The counselor had suggested she go back to school to get a bookkeeping certificate. But Anita had refused.

Her thoughts faded as someone tapped on the window. It was Janeva Babson, a young black woman who had come in two years earlier.

"Hi, toots!" Janeva called. "Why don't you join the mass march back to school?"

Anita answered gruffly, "Can't you see I'm on the slop-cleaning detail? Got work to do around this joint, you know. Costs a lot to keep us gals here in this fine, protected place. Gotta help pay our way!"

Janeva laughed. "What's the matter with you? Fleas in your bed last night?"

"Nothin's the matter that won't be cured in six months when I get out of here."

"Don't be too sure of that, honey-bunch!" Janeva warned. "That's only the day you go before the board. Even if they tell you that you can go, you still have to wait until your papers are all in order. Thirty days or more that takes! And you have to be a real good girl to get out in minimum time. I'm not so sure you're *that* good!"

Anita made a motion of tossing scrubwater toward Janeva.

Janeva laughed and dodged playfully. Then she got serious. "Think it over in a more positive way, Anita. This may not be such a good school, the kind you know about. But it's a damned sight better than the one I went to. I've found some real great teachers here. Had 'em last semester and I'll get 'em again. I've come up from second semester ninth grade to last semester of high school in two years here. How about *that*? I'll graduate in June. I'll send you an invitation, hand-engraved with my own personal nail file!"

Anita J. remained sullen. She refused to be reached, even by jolly, well-meaning Janeva.

"Get going! I'm tired of your sugar-coated success stories. It's a lot of hogwash, the whole business! A high school diploma isn't that important these days. How much do you think it's going to help *you*? Some high and mighty guy can still put you down. He'll find some way to do it if he doesn't like black people."

"Maybe," Janeva agreed sadly. "It could be like that. But Whitey won't be able to say, 'Sorry, beautiful, I can't hire you 'cause you can't come up with a high school diploma!' This time I'll have the fun of watching him squirm to find some other reason. And there's something else I'll have. Whitey can't take it away. Nobody can."

Anita looked up, allowing herself to be interested.

"It's knowing things," Janeva continued, "like reading along in a magazine, finding a sentence or so in French, and knowing what it says. Just like that. It's fun to know things—like biting into the best piece of chicken."

Anita had had enough. "Get out of my sight! Go on to that dumb school. I'll go on fighting slop!"

Janeva turned away from the window with a final "Think again, honey-bunch!"

Anita J. and Janeva B. represent the two extremes of educational ambition in all prisons. The Anita women give up, go on blaming everyone but themselves for their predicament. They continue to resist every effort to get them into a definite educational or vocational training program. Their test results show that they are capable of improving themselves. Sometimes they do start a rehabilitative program, but they lack the self-motivation to stay with it. Self-motivation is essential in prison.

The Janeva B. women come to accept their own responsibilities; they face up to what they must do to prepare for a new life.

When emergency situations occur, as they sometimes do, causing unforeseen interruptions to school or training programs, some of the women find it difficult to overcome the discouragement and frustration. The Anita J. types simply can't bounce back, study on their own, or take personal initiative for lesson preparation in spite of institutional interruptions. The same traits of character probably had a lot to do with their being in prison in the first place and will make parole violation almost a certainty. Perhaps one day a means can be found to reach these women in such a way that their attitudes and behavior can be changed.

Let's take a look at the educational background of residents in women's prisons in 1971. Reports from other such institutions in the United States show a general average from grade 5 to grade 10, with a few having a college background. The picture is much the same at CIW. However, as noted earlier, the newly committed resident often claims a grade level higher than test results indicate. Therefore, the rough average of grade 7-plus is probably a little high.

California Institution for Women reports a monthly inmate average of 590 for 1971. The grade level percentages are consistently much the same, with the greatest number at junior high level. This is not surprising, although chronologically these women are of course older than junior high when the gates clang shut behind them.

The junior high age is the big school drop-out age, the cop-out age. At that time the girls are twelve to fifteen years old, with no job skills, no specific goals. Also, it's the big 'want age,' when they want things that money can buy: cars, expensive music equipment, the 'right clothes' (whatever they consider right), color TV, liquor, and cigarettes, which most consider a necessity. Along with these desires is the aggressive determination to get everything they want *now*.

A girl without educational or job goals has a lot of time on her hands, time to go shopping, to look at things she can't afford. Shoplifting becomes one of the first steps toward greater crimes. She has time to explore the hangouts of the junkies, the pushers, the liquor-guzzling associates. Finally, she's involved in petty theft, in writing bad checks (she did learn to write before she quit school!). Her next step may be helping to steal cars, armed robbery, even manslaughter—or worse. The day comes when the crime is so serious that the state gives her one-way transportation to a state prison.

In the modern, progressive prisons the counselors and other staff members are generally quick to encourage the women to get into school and to work toward a realistic goal. Some get the point quickly, as Janeva did, and enroll in an educational or vocational program.

Others, such as Anita J., never get the point, or never apply it to themselves. They shuffle along from day to day, 'doing time,' trying to find new ways to 'beat the system.' In some cases these self-defeating attitudes do change. In others they only become hardened.

This is unfortunate, for the opportunity is there. The staff and administration admit there is much to be done to improve realistic training opportunities, but giant steps have been made in the last few years. All teachers are fully credentialed, and the program is parallel with its counterpart in the free world. In June 1971 twelve women received diplomas for high school graduation. Altogether there were 127 who reached an educational or vocational training goal recognized by the public schools of California. In addition, fifty received certificates of completion in creative dynamics. This is an inspirational type of self-analysis program that has been helpful to many. It is now being offered for credit.

Of the remaining 413 in California Institution for Women in 1971, many were working toward educational goals which they planned to reach during their term.

There are some who are so handicapped physically or mentally that they cannot take part in any program. At present there is little that can be done for the mentally handicapped in prison. Some of these should be in hospitals or training schools for the mentally ill, but budgetary cuts in such institutions, along with legal tangles of various kinds, keep them in prison.

The 177 who did reach a goal of self-improvement in 1971 are proving to themselves and others that they are making real progress toward their own rehabilitation. Some are on parole now, have found employment, and seem to be making a successful return to society. Each year there will be others who will reach goals of personal improvement, both educationally and in their attitudes. There will always be some who never will, no matter what. But in the beginning of incarceration the attitude must be that all can become independent, acceptable members of the world outside the gates.

All prisons offer educational opportunities through the elementary grades. Most offer high school. But the quality of the educational programs is not what it should be in all cases.

Eleven states offer college courses through correspondence or arrangement with local community colleges. States which make college available to inmates are Colorado, Delaware, Georgia, Illinois (to AA degree), Indiana, Iowa, Kansas, Minnesota, New Jersey, and New York.

Those who plan programs to be used within the various prisons for women have many ideas for enriching the programs already in operation, for starting new ones, for expanding the work furlough program and the vocational areas. Two prisons, Indiana and Massachusetts, reported plans to begin offering business courses in January 1972. One has a plan to offer computer training. CIW also has plans for program enrichment for 1972 in both academic and vocational areas.

But these ideas are only words on paper until money and trained personnel become available.

As mentioned earlier, the cost of keeping a woman felon in prison (CIW) for the year 1972 was $6,820. If there is any chance at all that a woman can become a useful member of society through an intensive training and counseling program, it will be an obvious economy. A long-termer can become a very expensive state property.

⊛⊛⊛⊛⊛⊛⊛⊛⊛⊛⊛⊛⊛⊛⊛⊛⊛⊛⊛⊛⊛⊛⊛

CHAPTER 6

INSTITUTIONAL WORK OR VOCATIONAL TRAINING— WHICH IS IT?

FOR THOSE who cannot fit into any academic program in the institution, vocational training may be the answer. This does not mean that vocational skills require no reading, writing, or arithmetic ability. On the contrary, how could a clerk-typist keep a good job if she couldn't read and spell correctly? Nurse's aides surely need reading skills just to complete their own job sheets.

But there are a few vocational programs that demand very little 'book knowledge.' At CIW, as in nearly all prisons reporting, institutional sewing is one of these. Let's take a look at Linda, who sits at one of the big power machines.

There are probably twenty women who work regularly in the industrial sewing building at CIW, each doing one thing over and over, her own small operation contributing to the finished product. Linda sews collars on blue cotton shirts.

A visitor from 'outside' stops at Linda's machine.

"What are you doing?" the visitor asks, trying to be heard above the noise of the machine.

"Putting collars on these damned shirts!" Linda yells back. "All day I sew collars on shirts."

"Is this your job training or your institutional work?"

"Both," Linda answers. With a shrug of indifference as if to say "Try to figure that one out!" she turns back to her machine.

Few of the women even look up from their work. They are used to people wanting to learn from one quick glance what a vocational program is like in a women's prison.

Linda is luckier than most. She is being paid for her institutional work. She started at 2¢ per hour because she already knew how to do this kind of work. After a certain number of hours on the job she received 4¢. Raises came at the end of stated numbers of hours of work until she is now at maximum, 19¢ per hour. The most a woman can earn in CIW is $16.50 per month. This is credited to her account and can be drawn on for personal purchases from the campus store. If there is any left when she is released she takes it as part of her release money. But the job preparation is the important thing, not the pay.

However, institutional sewing does not necessarily help women get good jobs after release. First of all, a woman must be paroled to an area that hires many workers in garment factories. Since garment factories are often located in the less desirable sections of big cities, there is another problem: such areas do not often provide a good environment for a parolee who wants to begin a new and better life.

A few prisons, such as Florida and Iowa, have an expanded sewing program that includes fine tailoring and alterations. As of January 1, 1972, the vocational sewing program at CIW includes an evening class that teaches pattern-cutting and custom design.

Laundry work is listed as a vocational course in twenty-four prisons. This is a mistake. With washing equipment what it is today, and the self-service laundries meeting the needs of the women without a home laundry, there is little demand for anyone to do work of this kind. Consequently, experience in a prison laundry just isn't much help in getting a job outside.

Institutional laundry is a hot, tiring kind of work which no one wants to do, but it must be done. Here again comes the conflict between true vocational training programs and the labor needs of any institution running on a twenty-four-hour basis. These needs are especially difficult to meet in places supported by tax money. Since July 1971 laundry has not been considered vocational training at CIW. It's called just what it is, institutional work.

Some prisons pay nothing for any kind of institutional work. Every inmate takes her turn at all the jobs within her abilities, like them or not. In a few weeks she has learned to do her work reasonably well. She can mop acres of floor space, polish the hospital hallways, manage the laundry equipment, wash stacks of dishes either by hand or by machine, help cook thousands of meals, mow the grass, trim the shrubbery and wash windows. All these tasks must be done and should be regarded as a necessary part of an inmate's learning to meet a job schedule. Also, it is only fair that each should take responsibility for paying part of the expense of her stay there. But all this does not alter the fact that few such duties carried out on an institutional basis will fit her for a job when she is released.

As to pay for institutional work, there seem to be many ways of handling this. At CIW the clerical jobs pay best, for they require skills the inmate probably had when she came. She may be placed in a job that will improve those skills, or she may be able to take related courses. Several CIW residents are now working in various offices as clerical assistants. Again, $16.50 per month is the top. Kitchen work is at the bottom. In some prisons no difference is made in jobs. The pay range is from nothing for any job to $2.40 per day, with a lot of steps between. One prison pays 10¢ per day for every job, or $3 per month to a release account. Whatever the rate of pay, no one in prison will be likely to play the stock market with her earnings when she gets out. Also, she almost never really handles money. Only seven prisons reported that inmates are allowed to handle money, either what they earn inside or money sent from the outside. In all other cases the money goes into the inmate's prison account as a credit toward purchase of personal need items. Or it is given to her in some form of scrip that has no value outside. Scrip may be a card to be punched with the amount credited or paper tickets in various amounts. One prison uses plastic pieces representing cash amounts.

In spite of the need for labor to keep the prison going, CIW has a program of janitorial training aimed at preparing women for domestic service jobs and for janitorial jobs for industry. A woman is encouraged to go that road if she and her counselor feel that this would give her a better chance for employment during parole. In 1971 fifteen women completed this course. There will be no way to learn whether this training was helpful until they have been outside for a while. It isn't easy to place women newly paroled in domestic service jobs, even when they are well trained for them. There are several reasons for this.

The prisoner may have personality problems that will work against her as a household employee. She may have had such serious difficulties with drugs or alcohol that she cannot cope with a domestic service job, especially in a private home. In that case a job with an industrial cleaning company would be preferable—except that there are so few of them. A man with a big machine can clean a dozen hotel rugs in less time than it takes a maid to change the linen in half that many rooms. As in practically all areas of work, the machine age has closed out many jobs for which the unskilled or even the semiskilled woman was once really needed.

If a woman is physically able and emotionally ready for work in domestic service she should be encouraged to prepare for it, although most such jobs pay only the minimum wage. But while she's working on a low-pay job she can always be watching for a better one or taking night school courses to prepare for it. A woman who is in the free world has the opportunity to move around and look for better employment. A minimum wage that is earned legally and is hers to spend as she will is better than no job—or a short-term, highly paid illegal one. If she can keep that thought in mind, it could mean the difference between staying free and returning to prison.

Most prison administrators are eager to enrich their vocational training programs. At different times particular vocational programs have been asked for by the CIW women, but only a few of the inmates are educationally ready or even interested. Also, it is difficult to get qualified teachers for highly specialized skills. Plus all this, administrators must justify every experimental move. "How many women will benefit? How many are ready for it?" the state asks. "What will it cost? Are jobs available in that field at a self-supporting wage?"

The nursing program at CIW showed great promise when begun in 1968. But for a variety of reasons it was temporarily stopped. However, the institution planned to begin (June 1972) a program for licensed vocational nursing (LVN). Two local hospitals are cooperating with this one-year program. Preliminary screening for the first class has already been done. CIW also offers nurse's aide and vocational nurse training. In 1971 forty-seven received the nurse's aide certificate and twenty-four the vocational nurse certificate. The latter is not to be confused with the LVN program, which requires the applicant to pass a state board examination.

Now seven states report a program for LVN training. They are California, Delaware, Iowa, Kansas, Kentucky, South Carolina and Texas. Twelve states report nurse's aide courses: California, Delaware, Georgia, Iowa, Kansas, Kentucky, Maine, Missouri, New Jersey, Pennsylvania, Texas and Wisconsin. West Virginia is beginning such training this year.

The very nature of the work presents difficulties for maintaining a good LVN program. When trainees go out to local hospitals for on-the-job experience, as most of them must, they are daily exposed to drugs of many kinds. No hospital has enough staff to supervise high-risk trainees. Women who are to receive this training and experience must be women who have never been involved in the drug culture or who have shown a completely clean record for quite a long time. Obviously it is not easy to find such women in prison today. Too many went down that road *because* of drugs. But because this work holds much promise for employment outside, many states are renewing efforts to make all their hospital training programs effective.

Cosmetology, listed as Beauty Culture by some states, was begun at CIW in 1960. It is offered at a few prisons and is a very popular course. Staff encourages women to get into this if they have ninth- or tenth-grade reading ability. Every woman wants to be beautiful, and many times a woman's whole outlook on life, her feeling about herself and her own worth have been improved through this kind of work. Twelve cosmetology students paroled from CIW received state licenses during the years 1960 through 1967. But only two completed the course in 1970. When the economy tightens and jobs are scarce everywhere, beauty salons join the luxury items for thousands of people. The number of state licenses granted each year is set according to employment needs. Since a paroled woman was at the bottom of the list already, she was very lucky if she was even allowed to take the state exam. However, late information indicates that state regulations are loosening and that some recent cosmetology graduates from CIW were licensed. They got very good jobs soon after beginning parole. So doors are opening for the woman in prison to help herself—too slowly, perhaps, but they *are* opening. Cosmetology graduates are now allowed to complete the course, apply for and receive their state license before parole. Interest in this course is expected to increase noticeably. Alabama, California, Florida, Indiana, Minnesota, Missouri, New Jersey, New York, Tennessee, Texas, and Virginia now offer such training. Florida seems to emphasize charm courses as an important step in helping a woman to regain her self-respect.

Landscaping was also part of the vocational program for a while at CIW. Sometimes called horticulture, it is still pursued in some prisons. The course has proved to consist primarily of yard maintenance, an occupation unsuited to women because much of it requires a kind of physical strength women don't have.

Ceramics, popular as a creativity course, was dropped from the vocational program at CIW because ceramics plants are found in so few areas of California, and these are not usually in the cities, where the parolees go. The department is still maintained, however, and the products

from it are sold through the art shop in the administration building, enabling a few women to add to their prison
release account.

The recently added key-punch course is an office-
related skill, as is business education, also new on the
list. With only six weeks given to key-punch training, it
remains to be seen whether such a short period of training is sufficient to prepare a woman to compete with those
trained outside for these jobs.

There are many problems in planning for a training
school. For one thing, the labor market changes. Workers
needed today may be too numerous when the woman is
paroled. Cost is another factor. To make it worthwhile,
administration must show a minimum of fifteen students
enrolled before a new course can be added. The suggested
course must also promise employment for the inmate
during parole and after. This isn't easy, especially when
jobs of all kinds are hard to find, even for people who
have never been in prison.

How does a paroled woman find a job in the free world?
Sincere effort to get employment of some kind is a condition of her parole, so she must waste no time.

There are some very helpful sources, such as Trade
Advisory Committees (TAC), made up of people in the
community. There is a Trade Advisory Committee repre-
senting each vocation. In California these groups have
been very active. Several states mention help through vocational rehabilitation programs. Sometimes local groups
and even interested individuals help, once they know the
problem and learn to accept their responsibility for people on parole.

One problem every parolee must solve is how to deal
with a prospective employer. If she tells her parole status,
she is often shown the EXIT immediately. If she doesn't
tell, the employer will probably find out anyway and feel

he's 'been taken'; then out she goes. Although many have received disappointing treatment for being honest, counseling policy is to urge the women to continue to give the basic facts at the very first interview. This is a very hard thing to do, for a paroled woman usually feels very insecure about even applying for a job; she feels the deck is already stacked against her. But revealing the truth about her background has generally proved to be the safer course. After she explains her situation she is cautioned not to pursue the subject further.

If the parolee has not made good use of her time in prison, if she closed her mind to all possibilities to improve her skills, she may have more trouble outside than she had inside. If Linda fits into this category, she will go on sewing collars on institutional shirts, maybe for her whole time in prison. She may get up to pattern design, but from there she has no place to go. She may really enjoy sewing. She may want to design and make clothes for children and have a little shop of her own. But how does she get started in a small business? Where does she go to find out? People without a prison record can often get small-business loans, but usually this door is closed to people on parole. She goes on with her routine sewing, learning to hate it as time goes by. Besides, there is no clothing factory in her parole area, so her hope of employment in that kind of place is small.

She may go back to her old job— 6 A.M. to 2 P.M. in ROSIE'S KOFFEE KUP. It's right in the middle of junkie heaven. Sooner or later a pusher will offer her a part of his take for getting new customers. In prison she learned some new ways to do it. Maybe the pusher's world is all there is for her. This time she might get away with it.

What is there to lose?

CHAPTER 7

SELF-HELP IN PRISON

Many prisons today are using various kinds of self-help programs within their confines. These are apart from or in addition to any religious services the women may choose to attend.

One of these programs at CIW is called creative dynamics. It is led by people from the free world who are well trained in psychology, group therapy and other areas of positive thinking. It was first given without credit, but in 1971 it was made a credit course.

The students in creative dynamics are led toward thinking about their chances for a better life; they are helped to face their problems realistically, to develop the strength to mean it when they say, "I have certain weaknesses which made me commit the act that brought me here. I may feel that I don't deserve the sentence I got, that I wasn't to blame. But I *was* to blame in one way or another. I am responsible for rebuilding myself so that I can become a positive member of society, not a destructive one."

Then the course gives definite steps to help the student toward developing a new and socially acceptable self-image. As a kind of group therapy guided by outsiders, this has been a very helpful class.

Students receiving certificates in creative dynamics are given definite recognition at CIW. Many of them have never before received any kind of diploma or certificate showing a worthwhile goal reached. Their families may attend the graduation ceremony; friends and interested counselors and teachers come.

The ages of the graduates range from girls still in their teens to grandmothers. One young woman, upon receiving her certificate, spoke briefly of her happiness in learning so many things about herself.

"I feel good," she said. "I know my weak points do not need to be with me all my life. That it is up to *me* to make the changes, and that I *can* do it. The people who lead us here don't just preach; they give us real things to do. Like when I first came, the lesson was on how to start. The leader said, 'You don't like a certain staff member? O.K. Tomorrow you see her coming. You go down that hall. Don't speak to her the first time. Look over her, around her, through her, just as you think staff looks at you sometimes. Don't look *at* her at all! But go down that hall where you will have to meet her.' O.K., I did it. I didn't drop dead. Neither did that staff drop dead. Next time, the leader gave us the second step. This time we were to go down a hall where we would meet this staff woman, and this time we would look *at* her. Make her look back at us, maybe she would even speak, but we didn't need to speak first. And so that's the way it was, step by step. Now I'm not afraid to meet any staff, any place, and most of the time we speak real friendly. There's one once in a while that just looks over our heads or through us. I go right to work on that person, and most of the time I find she's not really sour. She just had a bad night herself!"

This is what creative dynamics means to prison residents—help in recognizing their own personality problems, then facing them, then taking steps to change their own attitudes. Group therapy is similar to creative dynamics except that it is led by counselors or specially trained staff members. Women are not forced to take part in group therapy, but they are encouraged to do so; some inmates even say they are 'nagged' to do it. A new resident is often not up to group therapy, for it can get pretty rough. But as time goes on she can take it, and the results are usually positive. Hostilities can be brought out, talked about until they lose much of their importance. Sometimes these sessions reveal that the hostilities are based on a general prison problem and that conditions exist which need to be corrected from the top. Then the women have a chance to think and talk about ways to get staff to consider the changes they want and feel are reasonable.

At CIW these sessions are called 'grouping.' Inmates are given a definite time and place to meet. Sometimes a new inmate needs psychiatric treatment before she can respond to any kind of grouping. If for no apparent reason she does not make progress toward self-analysis through grouping, she may be given special counseling for a while. If she cannot be reached in any of these ways, then she just isn't a very promising prospect for rehabilitation.

Since the average case load for CIW counselors is 120, there isn't time for as much one-to-one counseling as is desirable. Other ways must be found to help the women work out new behavior patterns.

Besides the self-help programs already mentioned, some prisons have instituted a program called the 'Seventh Step.' Bill Sands, author of *My Shadow Ran Fast* and

The Seventh Step, after his release from San Quentin, organized prerelease training programs and worked on other kinds of self-help programs for prisoners. The Seventh Step has been in operation at CIW at different times, but one of the problems is that it depends so much on the ability and leadership qualities of the woman in charge, and too often the ex-con leader still has too many problems of her own. But it must be that way or it isn't the true Seventh Step plan.

One of the most successful self-help programs at CIW is carried out by a group called Prison Preventers, organized in the spring of 1970 by the inmates themselves. Thirty-five to forty women attend meetings regularly, with the role of the leader taken by a different woman each time. This rotation of leadership seems to help in keeping the program strong. Sometimes staff members attend the meetings. The organization includes many very intelligent women, most of whom accept the idea that their life style has not brought happiness either to themselves or to their families. When they become a part of Prison Preventers they admit that their former ways of handling themselves must be changed or they will never be ready for life in the free world.

There have been several instances in which Prison Preventers have worked in a positive way with grouping and also on an individual basis with disturbed inmates. Sometimes the prisoners know of a serious problem that has started small but is about to get out of hand. Staff may not know the problem even exists, or, if they do know, they may not realize that it is growing. Prison Preventers have been especially helpful in heading off serious racial conflicts and in preventing escape attempts. Sometimes they fail, but the threatened conflict is usually much less serious than it might have been had they not stepped in. When they fail, the prison code takes over: there is no 'snitching' about what happened at the Preventers meeting. Woe to the woman who breaks this code!

Let's look in on a meeting of the Prison Preventers:

The chairs are filled and some women sit on the gym steps. There is a feeling of waiting, of watching, a sense of a string pulled tight, almost to the breaking point.

Trudy Dawson takes her place as chairman. The waiting and the watching center on Trudy. A black girl who is not very tall and is usually shy does not carry much weight. But Trudy is different; the women listen to her.

Trudy is respected for many reasons. She had built a 'fence' organization and had helped all manner of thieves dispose of 'hot goods.' She had dealt with all races of people, with important thieves and unimportant ones. It takes a lot of 'smarts' for that kind of success. Trudy has proved her 'smarts' many times. Now she is here for a five- to ten-year term for her part in a huge stolen-goods operation.

But something had happened to Trudy in the last few months. Just what no one knew—perhaps not even Trudy herself. She was no longer interested in 'fencing'; she refused even to talk about her former successes.

She had helped organize a Prison Preventers group, and it is going well. The members are women who have good ideas about rebuilding their lives but often feel weak and hopeless. Sometimes the weak feeling becomes a real down-slide. Then they need each other.

Tonight they all need each other. Usually Prison Preventers is almost an even mix as to racial groups, but only two white women are present at this meeting. They sit near the door as if ready to run.

The trigger incident today was the transfer of a very disturbed black woman from her cottage to the psychiatric treatment unit (PTU). With a bongo-drumbeat on the table Trudy calls the meeting to order.

Excited, angry words begin to pour out. Trudy points
to one of the noisiest women.

"O.K., Ethel, you tell it. The rest of you shut up!" The
women become silent. Ethel speaks first.

Trudy is clever enough to give each speaker a chance
to talk. Then she summarizes all the talking, the yelling,
the joint talk.

"O.K., you agree that Skidoo is no angel. You have all
complained about her to the cottage supervisor because
she yells and cusses for nothin'. The soops [supervisors]
tried all kinds of easy things to settle her down. She
wouldn't cooperate, so they put her in PTU. She made it
real tough for C.O. Dugan [male custody officer], so her
room is all messed up. You think it should have been done
differently. Maybe, maybe not. You know Skidoo wasn't
going because they asked her to. You know her better
than that. First, you say they beat her with a chain. Then
it boils down to handcuffs. O.K., why did C.O. Dugan use
handcuffs? And somebody said he pulled her hair. Let's
bring it all out! You two white broads back there: Can't
you talk? You live in that cottage. What did *you* see?"

"If I say anything against Skidoo you black women are
going to beat on us. Maybe we better take the Fifth
Amendment!"

A few scattered laughs greet her statement.

"I promise no one will beat on you. You're a lot safer
here than you will be if this thing explodes. That's all
we're tryin' to do—keep it under control. You're a Prison
Preventer yourself. Come on, give!"

One of the white women whispers to the other. The
listener nods. The one who whispered to the other goes
up and stands beside Trudy.

"O.K., Trudy," she says. "I'm gonna *show* you what
happened.

"I was late coming from lunch and I walked right into

it. Trudy, I'm gonna bite your arm. It will hurt a little. You make me stop any way you can."

The room is deadly quiet. Not even a foot shuffles.

The woman bites down on Trudy's arm.

Trudy yells as she digs her free hand into the white woman's long blond hair, pulling her head up.

The biter opens her mouth, releases Trudy's arm.

She looks at Trudy, begins to cry. Smiling through her tears she says, "You played the game. Right along with me you played." Almost lovingly she pats the teeth marks she has made. "Sorry about that," she says.

Then she speaks to the whole group.

"That's what Skidoo was doing to Cat Dugan. Only she bit until blood was comin'. I saw it. What else *could* he do? That Skidoo is a wild one when she gets started. If she'd been lily-white and actin' like that, Cat Dugan would have done the same. I bit you real easy to show you how it was. You did what Dugan did—you pulled hair!"

A relieved kind of laughing begins to ripple through the group. They begin to talk among themselves about the incident. Someone laughingly remarks that there are lots of ways to hang onto a man, but biting isn't the best one!

After allowing a few minutes of soul-cleansing through talk, Trudy again calls for order.

"So, Prison Preventers, we've talked it over, we've looked at the whole thing. We've kept ourselves from getting write-ups for starting race trouble. Skidoo got what she needed—a room in PTU for a while. Let's hope she comes out a better woman."

Trudy says to the last speaker, "You're Chairman next time!"

The meeting breaks on a tone of friendliness. The tension is gone. Prison Preventers have come through another soul-searching session.

There are different types of self-help programs in all prisons, although the value of some might be questioned. The variety and quality will depend on the general attitude of staff and even as high up as the state officials. For all such programs, even though called 'self-help,' need the backing of those in control.

There are three strong ethnic organizations in CIW planned to help women of minority groups develop pride in their racial or ethnic backgrounds. SHAACO (Self-Help Afro-American Cultural Organization) has done much to upgrade attitudes toward black culture. An equally effective group is MARA (Mexican-American Research Association) for the women of Mexican-American background. They are interested in education, cultural understanding, and awareness of the role of the Mexican-American woman in our society.

According to the *Clarion* (published by and for CIW inmates), December 1971, another positive self-help effort is called the United Indian Tribes. This group "consists of fifteen to twenty Indian and other interested women, and has functions and goals similar to those of other ethnic organizations in the institution."

Some additional groups include: Narconen, based on scientology's approach to narcotics addiction; Daughters of Italy, a group of nationalistically identified women; Friends Outside, which brings men and women regularly to visit women residents who have no visitors; and Connections, a statewide concerned group of outsiders who provide help with transportation, passes, and family visits. Mothers Anonymous is a dynamic, meaningful group working to help child abusers change their behavior tendencies. The women's Toastmistress group, called Rhetoriques, is now going into its tenth year of successful meetings.

Altogether, CIW has thirty-one outside-sponsored self-

help groups meeting regularly. These include nine Prot-
estant religious groups and one Catholic. All prisons
reporting allow religious leaders to meet with inmates.

At CIW the Roman Catholic church provides a priest
on a part-time basis. He holds regular masses and has a
choir and a Legion of Mary group.

The American Friends Service Committee sends visitors to meet with the women, to provide the objective
listening ear to those who feel a need to talk to someone
other than a prison employee.

The religion of Islam is also represented, plus philosophy groups such as Yoga.

One of the religious workers commented that only
about 5 percent of the women in CIW claimed any special or strong religious faith when they came in. "We must
try to build into their thinking a kind of strength, a faith
that most of them just don't have; if they did, they probably wouldn't be here," he said.

In most prisons there are other self-help groups, such
as Alcoholics Anonymous and Narcotics Anonymous. In
all these groups, leadership is the key. A prison population is a coming and going thing. When a strong leader
leaves, the organization usually suffers a setback until
new leadership comes forward.

Inmate newspapers can also be a very fine self-help
activity. These papers give talented residents an opportunity to write creatively and to express their own views
on problems inside. They also learn the basics of news
reporting, illustrating, editing, layout, and other work
connected with publishing any kind of newssheet for
public reading.

Of the thirty women's prisons reporting, more than 50
percent have a regular newspaper. Although one of them
is rather closely censored (according to a report on the
questionnaire), it appears that most are allowed consid-

erable freedom of expression. Illinois and Massachusetts publish on an irregular basis. Alabama and North Carolina are beginning a paper. Wisconsin reports that this project was tried once but failed; no reasons were given. Thirteen prisons have no paper, nor do they have immediate plans for one.

A prison paper can also open new fields of vocational training. But this takes money, equipment, and trained leadership. It is encouraging that so many women's prisons already have a newspaper going or are starting one. It is certainly a step forward in developing public awareness of the existence of these several thousand American women behind the bars of felons' prisons. Perhaps more publicity through prison newspapers to the general public will bring about legislative support for improving all educational and vocational programs inside all prisons.

The self-help programs we have discussed can be of great value in any institution. However, like all programs that are matters of choice, they are just as effective as the people involved want them to be. To draw a parallel in the outside world, many communities have fine adult education programs. But taking advantage of them is a matter of choice. To work hard, to attend classes regularly means disciplining oneself. Some can and do; some won't and don't.

The same is true in prison, only more so.

~~~~~~

CHAPTER 8

INSIDE-OUTSIDE CONTACT

U<small>NTIL</small> quite recent years, inmates of prisons were locked away from practically all contact with the general public. Visiting was so carefully controlled that many who were inside saw only the employees and other inmates. From the day of commitment to the day of release they lived in a world of prisoner and keeper.

In most medium security institutions this is no longer true. Even in maximum security places there is some contact with people from the outside, the amount and kind depending on the individual case. With some residents, controls are not actually loosened but are maintained through honor systems of various kinds.

The honor system follows different routes. Work release, home furloughs for a job or family reasons, shopping trips into nearby towns, the seventy-two-hour pass, earned leave through some kind of merit system—all are forms of the honor system. Usually these privileges are granted near parole time to minimum security inmates.

Exceptions are sometimes made, especially with long-term prisoners who show much improvement in attitude and performance.

Freedom to choose to attend or not to attend one of the many evening activities is part of the honor system at California Institution for Women. One of the most important innovations approved by prison administrators has been the admittance of various kinds of entertainment and educational programs. The reason back of this is not to reward the prisoners, but to remind them that the world 'out there' is still rolling along, that there are people who do remember those who are not free to live outside a prison yard. Hopefully, the opportunity to see various types of entertainment will give them something to think and talk about besides their own troubles. This alone helps relieve the tensions that build in closely supervised confinement of any kind.

Because women as a group are usually appreciative and respond well to interesting happenings, in some prisons they get many opportunities to see plays, musical programs, special movies, and slide shows. Nearly all women's prisons reporting state that, as the schedule permits, guests and entertainment from the outside are welcomed; only one institution shows a highly restrictive policy. Band and singing groups are usually admitted; other types of performances are screened individually, the only standard being that of good taste. Inmates sometimes object to the 'good taste' restriction, saying this is censorship—which it is. The loss of choice in nearly all areas of life is the real punishment a woman suffers when she is committed to a felons' prison.

Crowd response in a prison may reveal facets of life middle-class America has not experienced. An example was the gun-juggling performance given at CIW. At the first shot the gym filled with shrieks, and around 90 percent of the women hit the floor; most of them were black.

A visitor sitting between two inmates, one white, the other black, said, "Now why did they do that? The guns are only loaded with blanks. They know that. But look at them—on the floor, scared to death!"

The black woman beside her said almost scornfully, "The way you say that shows you don't know much about the way most black people still have to live. When a big noise comes, we duck! Might be bricks a-flyin', or bottles, or guns. We run if we got time. When trouble happens in the streets, the police come, he arrests the black people first. Black people get killed first, arrested first, out last."

The women on the floor got up, adjusted their clothes, and laughed at each other, a bit embarrassed.

The 1970 and 1971 high-spot entertainment for CIW residents was the circus, attended by all who were able to go or allowed that much freedom. Visitors who happened to be present mingled with the inmates, laughing clapping, a part of the circus spirit.

Besides the delights of the circus, there were hot dogs, soft drinks and cotton candy.

It was a beautiful little glimpse of the outside, with the loosely rolled barbed wire along the rooftops the only reminder that after the show some would be completely free, others not. The circus people went their way, taking with them the magic, leaving the reality of the prison world. The inmates returned to the old routine, the feed lines, the 6:00 P.M. count. But for a time it would be easier to live with it.

Nearly all prisons now encourage volunteer workers, especially those who will share creative skills with inmates; teachers are welcomed. Some institutions require a training period for volunteer workers. Others simply base their decision on the background and qualifications and the personality of the would-be worker. In this area much more could probably be done and no doubt will be as the general public becomes better informed about prison life.

Sometimes college classes, service clubs and various civic groups come in. These contacts are helpful in developing public understanding and at the same time giving the women a glimpse of the outside world.

Often these groups come in after dinner, as working people usually cannot get away during the day. They come to the reception desk to be checked in. A list of contraband objects and materials is posted on the desk and reads as one would expect: No drugs, no cigarettes, candy, gum, food of any kind; no knife, gun, camera or tape recorder.

Purses must be left in waiting room lockers; no packages may be taken in. Every individual must present the palm of his hand for the black ink stamp. The custody officer at the reception desk counts the number of people going in. This must agree with the number coming out. It would be hard to imagine anyone's wanting to stay inside, but there have been incidents in the past which make the out-count step necessary.

Sometimes, in spite of these rules and the watchful eyes of the desk C.O. and others, forbidden things do get in. Now and then drugs are found after a large group has visited. The only way to prevent this would be to make a complete body search of every visitor. Obviously, this is impossible, nor would it be desirable if it could be done. If drugs or other contraband items are found after visitors have left, the women receiving them get the write-ups, something none of them wants. Perhaps those in authority feel that an occasional temptation is a good strengthening exercise for a resident. The world outside is full of opportunities to 'mess up' again. The inmate's ability to stand up to an occasional exposure is an indication of her readiness to meet the world outside, to cope with complete personal freedom. This is not to say that any warden or custody officer would deliberately put stumbling blocks in the way of the women; but rather that some degree of laxity exists because staff realizes there is a point beyond which they cannot control the behavior of women in their care, particularly those in minimum custody.

Some inmates are allowed to go outside for special reasons. Now and then a group goes to a nearby college to 'rap' with sociology classes. Especially able speakers may go to service clubs—if they are in minimum custody. Now and then an exception is made, and a maximum custody woman is given this privilege—if staff believes she can handle it.

Sometimes women receive money from families. The limit at CIW is $40 per month, which is placed in her account. However, most of them receive much less than that, and some get nothing. But even though they have very little money, a shopping trip is a great event; at Christmas time it is a coveted privilege.

When the holiday season comes, women in prison, like women everywhere who are separated from their families, long for them and for their children. The women at CIW go to great lengths at Christmas to decorate their small rooms in a variety of colorful, creative ways. They enter enthusiastically into the plans for Christmas parties given for the children who come to see their mothers. If they themselves have no children coming, most of them are eager to help others who do have. Some of them dress dolls; some make stuffed toys or knitted and crocheted gifts.

Although they may have been among the world's poorest mothers outside, when Christmas comes, the prisoners' longing for their babies is especially sharp. If they qualify for a shopping trip, Christmas is the favored time.

There wouldn't be much in stock at a prison commissary that a small child would want or could use, so this time the inmate goes outside for a few precious hours. It's a privilege given only to those who have earned it, who appear to be ready, for the woman who goes with a counselor to shop has a terrible temptation to cut and run. The counselor knows this and usually faces it realistically.

Let's look at Jane L., a minimum security resident chosen to go Christmas shopping for herself and for others who are not allowed to go.

Jane had served two years of a five- to fifteen-year term, a sentence earned because of her part in an armed robbery. When the big adventure started, she didn't know a gun would be mixed up in it. When she found out, it was too late.

Her boyfriend had said, "You hold the gun, and if that little kike storekeeper gives me any lip about opening the safe, you shoot! You hear me?"

"What if I hit him?"

Boyfriend had laughed scornfully. "You won't. You haven't hit a target yet!"

Luckily Boyfriend was right about her shooting ability. Just as the storekeeper began to turn the dial on his big old-fashioned iron safe, a cop appeared from out of nowhere.

Jane panicked. She pulled the trigger—and missed. So, instead of the gas chamber, she got a five- to fifteen-year sentence. She had been a cooperative prisoner, for, unlike many inmates in a felons' institution, she was a 'first timer,' not an experienced criminal of several years. She was just a kid looking for a thrill. Pulling a job in a small, isolated grocery store looked like fun.

Her fun had ended the night it began, and here she

was, within six months of parole, getting her first look at the outside in two years.

She had spent all her spare time for two days getting ready for the trip, washing and setting her hair, borrowing clothes and accessories so she would look just right.

Jane and the counselor came back laden with bundles.

When Jane told her pals about the trip she said, "I could have cut out several times, but you know something? I couldn't afford to. I had a lot too much I might lose. So here I am to finish my stretch."

The occasional shopping trip is one facet of an honor system that is being employed to prepare the inmate for release. More and more prison directors are following some type of plan to expose their charges to segments of the free world before allowing them to tackle the whole thing. This is all a part of the necessary inside-outside contact.

Those inside are reminded that the so-called free world has a lot of restrictions, many of which they have forgotten. The experience is also good for people outside for they also have to make decisions. When the prisoner goes shopping, local store clerks usually recognize her counselor as a prison employee, so it is not difficult to identify the young woman with her. Contact with those who must learn to make good judgments on many of the simple details of living is a good experience for people in the free world.

Another means of inside-outside contact now being utilized by twenty-five prisons for women is the work release or work furlough program. This program is regarded as one of the most successful innovations. State rules vary, but in general a woman must be on minimum custody and must be within six months of parole. She is carefully considered from all angles before she is allowed to participate. She is responsible for getting to her job and back on time. She must shun former associates who may have been her crime helpers; she must stay away from drugs and alcohol, the two biggest reasons why a parolee 'goes on the lam.' She eats and sleeps at the prison, continues to live within its rules. Work release is somewhat like wading in cold water before you plunge from the diving board.

People outside who employ a woman on work release or parole also have a good learning experience. It isn't easy to be patient with employees who must be told every move to make, who seem unable to make up their minds on ordinary everyday matters.

It takes a great deal of tolerance on both sides to make a work release program successful. In a few cases the program is so new that results cannot yet be shown. But all wardens reporting believe that this plan is one of the most promising to date.

It's true that some prisoners on leave through one of the forms of the honor system simply do 'walk-aways'— do not return to the institution. The temptation not to return to those confining buildings is just too much, especially if they are doing well in their work. However most 'walk-aways' end up returning, usually very soon. They have left without plans for living outside and quite often drift back because they have no place else to go.

The results of a walk-away can be very unpleasant. An escapee sometimes goes at once to old friends and is soon in trouble again, sometimes with a sentence for a new crime. She may return to prison pregnant or with a starter case of VD. She may get drunk or drug-stoned and have to be brought back. Barring these possibilities, she will sooner or later be spotted by a parole officer. If the P.O. 'runs a tight ship' she will probably see that the walk-away returns to prison at once. If the P.O. is more flexible, she may ignore the situation if the escapee has a job, seems to be fitting into free society, and gets into no further trouble. But the chances of this happening are small, and there is always the gamble that at some far-off time the whole thing may catch up with her.

In spite of the problems and risks involved in the honor system, the tendency now is to use it wherever possible as a means to encourage self-improvement. The inmate who comes back has shown she can handle limited freedom; she has proved to herself and staff that she is ready for the long haul of parole.

CHAPTER 9

WHAT IS PAROLE?

THE WORD 'parole' means different things to different people: It depends on where you sit! It's a privilege a prisoner must earn by showing that he is willing to manage his own life in socially acceptable ways. Successful completion of a parole term shows that the individual has been 'rehabilitated,' at least to the extent that he can keep out of trouble.

The first date a prisoner marks on her calendar is the day she goes before the California Women's Board of Terms and Parole. One moment she dreads the day, the next moment she can hardly wait. There are many restrictive conditions a parolee must accept and live with, for in some ways parole is really only a relaxed continuation of prison. The supervision is less stringent, but it's still there. However, even the unhappiest paroled woman usually agrees that parole is much better than prison. Now and then there is an exception to this when a woman has so many bad experiences during her first

weeks outside that she becomes actually terrified that she
may commit another crime and asks to be returned to
prison, where she knows the boundaries and has learned
to cope with them. She is then allowed an extra thirty days
in prison, during which time she may get more counseling. And she has a place to eat and sleep without constant
worry about the bill. However, this cancels out her parole
review; she must start her parole term all over. But her
little visit has reminded her that prison is really not a
good place to be. So she stiffens her backbone and at the
end of her thirty days goes out to tackle the world again.
California is the one of four states with a women's board,
a parole board to hear women's cases only. The California Women's Board is composed of five people, three
women and two men. The chairman is always a woman,
and all are political appointees. Thirteen other states also
use an appointment system which has political connota-
tions.

Under California's law a convicted felon is sentenced
to prison "for whatever term is prescribed by law." This
is called the "indeterminate sentence.' Many inmates feel
that it is unfair; they believe they would do a better job of
self-improvement if they were given a straight term with
no uncertainties. The Department of Corrections contends
(and experience seems to bear this out) that the indeterminate sentence gives a reward for good behavior, an
incentive for going to school, for learning a new skill, for
taking part in some of the self-help programs inside.

In California's law of the indeterminate sentence, each
crime carries a penalty with a set minimum and maximum. For instance, armed robbery carries a penalty of
five to ten years. If found guilty, the accused must serve
the minimum time of five years, but she may serve half
of it on parole. If her crime carries a one- to three-year
term, she is eligible for parole consideration at the end of

six months, half the minimum term. Near the end of the six months she appears before the Women's Board of Terms and Parole.

The Department of Corrections in California is now starting a policy that will change several things in that state's prison parole system. The reforms are the first of a kind nationally. They attempt to combine the good points of the indeterminate sentence with the advantages of giving inmates definite release dates. Instead of waiting for years, most inmates will know within six months of their conviction when they can expect to get out of prison.

However, to benefit from this change the inmate must do certain things: for example, he must get a high school diploma in prison or complete a prison trade school course or therapy program.

Prisoners who do very well are eligible to have their dates advanced. That is, they may be released earlier than the time originally set. Those who fail are subject to a postponement of their release dates.

It is hoped that this change will give more prisoners the incentive they have needed to develop the self-discipline they were sorely lacking.

At present there is considerable negative feeling because no black person serves on the parole board. Since more than one-third of the women at CIW are black, it seems there certainly should be one member who understands the special problems of black women. Now that black people are gaining in political strength, this situation could change at any time. Seventeen states already have at least one minority race member on their parole boards.

The Parole Board in California meets at CIW two weeks out of each month to talk to women nearing the end of their minimum sentence. If the woman has a good 'jacket' (record) and no serious write-ups; if she seems to have acceptable plans for life outside, and a family to receive her; if her general attitude shows improvement; if she has made a serious effort to gain educational or vocational skill—she will probably be given a parole date.

Then the paper work begins. The counselors know their women quite well. They know which ones have good 'jackets'; they also know which ones will probably be 'shot down.'

If a woman is 'shot down'—told that she isn't ready for the free world, that she must serve more time inside—the news travels fast on the prison grapevine. Her friends gather around, cry with her, curse the board, profane the whole system.

The 'shot down' woman dries her tears; she spends a few hours (or days even) in sullen thought. She has been told that she will be seen again in six months. In that time she will do one of two things: she will try sincerely to keep out of trouble, go to school regularly, do her institutional work better. Or she will try to learn tricks and mannerisms which she thinks may influence the board in her favor. She will get a lot of advice on that score. Far too many of these women have been before the board again and again. They have been on parole, have gone on the 'lam' (violated the conditions of their parole), may even have committed another crime. Here they are again. The board becomes accustomed to seeing the same faces. Recidivism, or return to prison from parole, runs at about 37 percent with California women felons. Much of it happens during the first months out, when there are so many difficulties to overcome.

Now to the woman who was not 'shot down.' She has had a successful hearing; she has renewed hope, a real goal, new meaning in the day's routine.

While the paper work goes on she may be given a seventy-two-hour pass to look for a job, to make living arrangements if she has no family ties. She may already have been on the work release program. If she is lucky, she has been on a job that will be permanent when she is released.

The paper work for release can usually be done in about thirty days; sometimes it takes longer. The parole officer (P.O.) in the area in which the parolee will work has received a pre-parole file on her. The P.O. makes a field investigation: that is, she verifies the information the inmate has given to the board. She makes her report to the institution, offering her judgment as to whether the woman's plans are likely to work out successfully. The P.O. wants the women who come to her area to make good on parole. She does *not* want to see them go back to prison, for it's her job to keep them out. To enhance the chances of a good parole, the P.O. may do a rather close field investigation. She looks for answers to such questions as: Does the woman have a job waiting for her? If so, is it likely to last? How many people will depend on her earnings? Since most of the women have children, the family situation will be looked at closely. On an average, three to four persons are state charges while a woman is in prison. Will she be ready to take on so many responsibilities when she gets out? Or will their demands and needs be so overwhelming that she may literally fall apart? If she is married, is her husband still around? If not, is he likely to appear and make life more difficult? If he is still her husband and in the woman's parole area, will he help her do a good parole? The parole officer must consider all these things and make her recommendation on her findings.

Perhaps the woman wants to go to a halfway house. Her work release job hasn't given her much hope for longtime work. She is afraid. She needs a refuge during these first very difficult weeks. She longs to be outside, but she's been dependent on an institution for a long time, and now she's just plain scared. And after reading that parole sheet again she realizes she still must live her life according to strict rules. It won't be easy. She needs a step between, which is what the halfway house is meant to be.

So her P.O. makes the arrangements with the halfway house. California has several, ranging from almost worse than nothing to excellent. A woman pays a low fee for board and room and may stay for as long as three months —or longer, if an extension could mean the difference between making a good parole and not making it. However, most women are eager to get out on their own and usually try hard to find employment to make this possible. State welfare or other forms of aid pay the cost if a woman has no money. In some cases churches and service clubs have stepped in to give a helping hand. The halfway house plan is gaining in use. Eighteen prisons for women report expansion of this program for helping a woman take the step from complete supervision to no guidance at all except her own will and judgment.

One big problem with the halfway house plan is that its success depends so much on the personality of the director. A halfway house needs a woman whose own background gives her a real understanding of a paroled woman's problems, who is strong in her own self-direction, who has leadership qualities and the personality to win and keep the residents' faith. Also, the director must be able to work with many points of view. Such people are not easy to find.

When the paper work is done and the plans all made, checked and approved, the woman has one last session with her counselor.

Reading the conditions of parole, knowing they actually apply to her, she sometimes goes into panic.

The counselor goes over the parole conditions with her.

"You mean I can't even leave town without the P.O.'s permission?"

"You must tell her your plans if you will be crossing county lines. If she advises against it, you'd better listen. She won't send a cop to stop you, but if you go and get into something you can't handle, you've had it! You'll most likely become one of those who come back here on a sort of swinging door plan—in and out, in and out."

The counselor points out other items. "You've had an alcohol problem, as many have. Booze is *no* for you, any kind of alcoholic drink. Look at Item 11, civil rights. You lost all that when you were convicted of a felony."

"Can't even get married until I finish parole. But I *could* shack up with a guy. O.K.?"

"That isn't exactly what Item 12 says," the counselor answers. "You can go to your P.O., and if you can show that marriage to a particular man would give you a home, more financial security, and loving help, I'm sure the P.O. would take steps to get that part of your civil rights given back to you."

"But I'd have to ask, like a sixteen-year-old kid. I'm twenty-five years old!"

"Yes, you'll have to ask. Some of your actions are still juvenile at times. Better keep working on that! And don't forget to send in that report sheet every month."

The parolee strongly resents having to ask permission for every act of importance. Although the P.O. will usually grant permission for any request that seems reasonable and has promise of a good outcome, it's having to *ask* that irritates the about-to-be-paroled resident.

Like so many good things in life, civil rights are not really appreciated until they are lost. Probably black women are better able to accept this loss than is the average Caucasian, because until recently the term had little meaning for American blacks, because it was a benefit that didn't apply to them.

When parole is successfully finished, a woman must make application to the governor for the restoration of her civil rights. In California this is called a Gold Seal Pardon. After a woman receives it the law has no more hold on her. All that remains of her experience are the memories. But all the Gold Seals in the world will not erase the memories.

~~~~~~

CHAPTER 10

NEW FACES

$\mathcal{S}$OME KINDS of illness are easy to see; some must be hunted down and treated. This is just as true where prison residents are concerned as it is with any other group of people. In fact, prison inmates usually have even more than their share of chronic physical problems. Some of these may have been caused by a childhood spent in real poverty with seldom enough to eat, with clothes totally unsuited to the weather. In the case of middle- to upper-income people, perhaps too little attention was given to providing the right kind of growing-up situation.

Perhaps a woman prisoner bears unsightly physical marks because of the way she has lived: for example, track marks from too many 'fixes' with the drug needle; she may have a displaced nose, a face scarred as a result of venereal infection, unsightly knife scars from actual fights. She may carry permanent burn marks, or her face may be a network of scars from traffic accidents that were somehow the result of her criminal activities.

Or a prison resident may be crippled for a reason over which she had no control. She may have been born with a physical defect which kept her body from growing straight, with buck teeth, or a jaw that makes her face look weak and unattractive. Any of these individual problems may have something to do with a woman's becoming a criminal. It is true that many people rise above physical defects of the most serious kind, seeming all the stronger because of their handicaps. But a closer look at the lives of such people will usually reveal a warm, loving family unit, enough money to get medical care when needed, a community that cares.

Women in prison do not usually come from a loving, understanding home or community. Add to that a serious physical defect, and the woman faces problems which to her seem hopeless.

Prison officials recognize the fact that it is very important to women to be attractive, not only to men but to other women, to possible employers, to society in general.

Of course, not all CIW residents committed crimes because they were physically unattractive. Many are very beautiful, keep themselves well-groomed, have a great deal of that elusive quality called charisma, or charm. In those cases their loveliness may have been part of their problem. Perhaps they learned when quite young how to use their charm in selfish, harmful ways.

But we are concerned now with the woman who can be helped to a better way of life by improvement in her physical appearance.

In modern, progressive prisons for women a great deal of effort is made to correct any physical defect residents may have. At CIW the first, careful physical examination usually discloses conditions that can or cannot be corrected. The report becomes a part of the inmate's file.

Take Ruth G., who sat in the counselor's office, her slightly twisted face a mask of sullen indifference.

Counselor W. talked about the various test results, putting in occasional remarks about the meaning of the record. She tried in many ways to get some kind of response to what was stated in the report, but Ruth G. remained an overweight blob.

Counselor W. gave up at last. "Well," she said, "it seems you're not ready for help of any kind. Maybe a few group sessions will do something for you."

Ruth G., inmate No. 1234, gathered herself together and spoke. Her voice had no life, no personality in it.

"You're wastin' your time," she said. "All you in this joint is wastin' your time. Look at my face! What man is gonna marry a woman that looks like me? Sure, he might go to bed with her if it's dark enough and he's not much himself. And who would give me a job, lookin' like this?"

"It's something that . . ." the counselor began.

Ruth G. interrupted, aroused now to some degree of action.

"Save your damn breath! Sure it's my fault! I should never been in that bar, drinkin' my fool head off. I know all you're gonna say. But it don't help me now! And nothin' you can say will help, either." She turned toward the door.

Counselor W. stepped firmly between Ruth G. and the door. "Sit down!" she commanded. "Now that you're talking, maybe you will listen to what I wanted to tell you." Accustomed to tones of command, Ruth G. sat down.

"I started to say that there is a way you can get help for your problem, right here. We have a fine doctor who can straighten that nose. He's rebuilt noses a lot worse than yours. Last year he did five face-lifts, and five women left here with a whole new outlook on life. If you want it done, our doctor can fix that nose like new, and there won't be any ugly scars. Now, what you do about the scars inside your head . . . that's mostly up to you, although we'll help all we can."

For the first time in her six weeks at CIW Ruth G. allowed her face to show a spark of life.

"You mean that?" she asked. "Don't say it if you don't mean it!"

"I mean it. I'll see the doctor tomorrow and we'll get you in as soon as possible."

So Ruth G. became one of the fifty-four CIW inmates in 1970 who had their noses made over. Ruth's surgery was not easy, and there was pain. No one could spare her that. But her new face was the beginning of a whole new set of attitudes toward her imprisonment.

Not all women undergoing cosmetic surgery can tell stories of tremendous change for the better. Sometimes too many other negative factors are involved, such as a resistance to anything recommended by the institution. Perhaps the woman has had many bad drug trips and knows that she may never be cured of addiction. So why go through pain to remove an outside problem when the inside one remains? Anyway, she argues, I have no family, nobody who cares what I look like. Why bother?

Nor will all prisons give much attention to a woman's need for personal physical improvement. There are so many more pressing problems demanding a part of their very limited budget.

Also, the attitudes of those responsible for the inmates must lean heavily toward rehabilitation; they must be not only willing but eager to cooperate with any plan that will send these women back to society in much better condition than when they came. Prisons without hospitals, with only part-time medical people or on-call doctors, will be very unlikely to have either the time or the facilities to do repair work. Only sixteen of the thirty women's prisons that reported have hospital facilities within the institution. Of this number seven report that they have a full-time doctor. Just how many of the seven are equipped to do physical repair work is not known.

Besides having facilities and staff to carry out cosmetic treatment, the people who pay the state bills for the support of prisons must be convinced that their investment will pay off. One can almost hear the protests:

"So now they want us to pay more taxes to fix those women up to be movie stars! My niece was in an auto accident, got her face cut up. Who paid *that* bill? We did, of course! Let those women behave themselves, serve their time, get out and go to work so they can pay their own face-lift bills!"

Such remarks show a lack of knowledge and understanding of the problem, one of the big blocks to prison reform. The speaker *is* going to pay the bill, one way or another. He should consider ways to reduce it. In California it costs $6,820 plus to keep a woman in prison for a year. If a woman with a disfigured face or a crippled body comes back to society with the same physical problems, plus the inside scars of a prison term, chances are she will again present the taxpayer with a bill of $6,820 plus per year. The record shows that 90 to 98 percent of imprisoned women will one day live among us again. Will they be better equipped to live a self-supporting, constructive life?

Cosmetic surgery isn't the only kind of repair work done in a modern prison hospital, although it is important, as any woman who has had an unsightly tattoo or ugly visible mole removed can tell you. Besides the nearly 300 cases treated in 1971 to improve appearance, several women had crippling conditions corrected. A damaged heel bone can be a serious handicap. Two CIW women can now walk normally because of this kind of repair.

Many women had dental work done which improved not only their appearance but also their general health.

This is not to say that the way a woman can get much needed medical attention is to commit a crime! Balanced against this possible medical help is the constant fact that, although she is a hospital patient, she is also still in prison. She must continue to live within the restrictions of prison. She may go out with a greatly improved physical body, and this is all to the good. But she will have the emotional scars of prison which the best medical people in the world cannot remove.

She may be called an inmate, a resident, a client, or a patient, but she is still a prisoner.

The personal bill for a prison term runs very high.

CHAPTER II

THE BUS RIDE OUT

THE LAST X has been marked on the calendar. Mary B. has served her time inside. Now she must finish the term outside, through parole. Some inmates feel that this policy needs change. They believe a shorter but predetermined sentence would be much better for all concerned.

A few inmates believe that there should not be a parole period at all, and there are prison officials who feel that the women's reasons should receive consideration. Others hold that parole is a necessity because some ex-cons are likely to become violent if suddenly given complete freedom; parole is a protection society must retain. There is definitely a move in most states toward shorter terms in prison, with the remainder of the time served on parole. Many women have been spared a return trip by a firm but understanding parole officer. On the other hand, a P.O. can run too tight a ship, and this can be another kind of problem for both the P.O. and the newly released woman.

Many women become so used to institution routine that they are just not ready to take life 'cold turkey' when they are released. They need an in-between step, a time to get a job and a place to live, to find new friends; a time to test their own strength, to learn to accept family responsibilities again. The halfway house idea is growing in popularity and is used as the in-between step by eighteen states.

But whatever lies ahead, most of these women will eventually leave prison behind. Some of them may have saved the money they received from family and friends, the money they earned from work inside or on work release. CIW women are given $68 when they leave, if their own assets are under $200, but this must cover transportation to their area of parole. They may have needed to buy clothes as well, although most women have been buying clothes from time to time. The luckier ones have had things sent to them by family or friends.

Sixty-eight dollars isn't much money with which to start a new life under any conditions. To live on that amount (even if they can keep every penny of it) until their first paycheck comes in is asking too much of anyone, particularly in times of inflation.

Sometimes a woman can get a loan from a service organization or church or from the halfway house. She may be going home to a family able and willing to help. If so, she is lucky. Too many will return to a welfare environment and will soon be welfare cases themselves, beginning again a treadmill of dependency.

Policies on release money (agate money) vary widely from state to state. One state gives only bus fare back to the point of conviction, plus any balance in their prison account, while three others give $100 and whatever is left in the prison account. If the inmates have had paying jobs inside and were very careful (no smoking, few cosmetics, minimum clothing), they may have saved some money. But at salaries ranging from zero to $2.40 per day for a few highly specialized jobs, no one will have a big bank account.

The woman about to be released has longed for this day. If she failed her first parole hearing, she has probably developed some deep feelings of hostility. If she has been cut down by staff members with less education than she has, she will no doubt carry a deep bitterness that will be no help on parole.

If she was pregnant when she went in, she may be looking forward to having her baby with her. If, however she gave it up for adoption, which few do nowadays, she may never see it again.

The young woman who came in full of hate toward everyone, who little by little was brought into the routine of a completely controlled life, is going out. She has been a non-person so long! Can she learn to be a person again, one accepted by the community to which she must return?

The bus is coming. No big deal has been made of her going. Her counselor has had her papers ready, helped her get her release money, told her that her parole officer would probably meet her. "But if she can't make it, just call this number and someone there will tell you what to do. Good-by, Mary, and good luck. Don't come back here now, you hear? Anyway not in a police car!"

Mary smiles, trying to look very brave, a woman of the world, but she is by no means sure of herself.

Settling into the bus seat, she looks back. She can barely see the barbed wire rolling along the top of the roof. Mary has both feared and anticipated this day. Now she is scared. Can she make it 'out there'?

Old associates will be after her, urging her to join the gang again. This will be especially hard to resist if she was convicted on a narcotics charge.

Her family may be embarrassed about having her return. And if she doesn't have a good job she will be just another mouth to feed.

She has little money left after buying her bus ticket to her parole area. She had bought a new dress with what was left in her prison account. She is luckier than most, for some prisons seem to take little or no responsibility for seeing that newly released prisoners have any money at all when they leave.

At her own request, Mary B. will stay for a maximum of three months at PREP (Pre-Release Environmental Preparation) House in Sacramento. She has come to realize herself that her family won't give her the help she needs to walk a straight road. Hopefully, at the end of the three months or less in PREP House she will have a job. She will have met and conquered some of the temptations that usually shadow a parolee. She will have learned that once she has said no to an exciting but dangerous invitation it is easier to say no the next time. In the meantime, she will have made friends with people who wanted her to make a good parole.

Another fear comes into her mind, crowding out other worries. Will people accept her, an ex-con, as someone who really wants a better life than the one she lived before she was sent to prison?

Will the parole officer meet her? She hopes so. The women who knew her said the P.O. she was getting was jolly and really straight, but fair.

Yet with all the hazards, both real and imagined, she is eager to go, to try to be a part of the free world again. With all the help she had received, it had still been a prison. She had had no privacy. All her mail was read;

she remembers that flashlight beam pushing through the
slit in the door at 10:00 P.M.; signing out for every activity, every change of location through the whole day;
seeing the custody officer come in to see if she got where
she was supposed to go; getting permission for every
move she made.

In spite of the growing openness, the new policies on
work furlough and 72-hour leave, family visits and all
that (and what if you didn't have any family who cared?),
it was a prison, and she was never able to forget it, not
for one moment.

When the bus reaches her parole destination she gets
off, mingles with the crowd. Whether the parole officer
has met her or not, she is again a part of the general public. This is the point where the citizen's responsibility begins. Let us look at the cold facts of the newly paroled
woman reentering free society.

In California every woman on parole costs the state
$600 to $900 per year depending on the amount of special
care needed. This is much better than paying $6,820
per year to keep her in prison, but it is still a bill of $50
or more per month presented to the taxpayer for every
woman on parole. It is to our financial advantage to do
all we can to help her make a good parole.

Society in general may or may not have been responsible for providing the environment which caused
this woman or any other female parolee to commit the
crime that sent her to prison. But we *are* responsible for
what happens while she is in a felons' prison. Her behavior patterns must be changed while she is there. If
they are not, she is likely to become a constant state
liability, in and out of prison.

Outside people must work closely with those responsible for the custody and training of those inside. The free
people must face the fact that anything connected with

prison will cost a lot of money. The big question is: shall state legislatures be urged to budget more generously to support rehabilitative programs both in and out of prison, or shall we do nothing except build more prisons when circumstances force us to do so? Either way will cost, not only in money but in time given to honest soul-searching for the right answers.

In some prisons the trend is toward making long-overdue changes. In March 1972 a very promising system was put into operation in the Women's Reformatory in Rockwell City, Iowa. Called Achievement Motivation, it is the result of long study and planning. If successful in Iowa, it could mean a giant step toward rehabilitation of inmates of other institutions who up till now have not responded to any standard educational program.

The basic idea is to motivate or move the prisoner (called 'client' in Iowa) to want to achieve a goal. People who work with many kinds of training programs realize that education has little value unless the individual really wants it. Achievement Motivation is defined as a set of feeling and action programs that will make the individual *want* to work for excellence.

The training session for achievement motivation is attended by both staff and clients and is aimed toward helping each woman take responsibility for the direction of her own life. Through this program each woman will be able to set her own goals, however simple or complicated they may be. Then she is helped through counseling and many kinds of training programs to reach her goal.

Many very interesting classes are being offered to provide more ways to achieve success. The entire program is planned to help every woman succeed at *something*. Most classes are kept to six weeks to hold attention and avoid discouragement. In this way a woman can attain a goal in a short time, whether it be finishing a dress or molding a ceramic figure. Then through various kinds of gradual exposure to community-based programs she can make her way toward parole and free society. Hopefully, she will be ready.

APPENDICES

When this book was first begun, it was intended to be the story of the California Institution for Women, a progressive modern prison. As the writing went on, the question naturally arose: If this is what life in a progressive prison is like, what is it like in a backward one?

The publishers felt that an effort should be made to gather information on a national level. This was done by means of a questionnaire that went out to the superintendent, sometimes called warden, of each prison that has separate facilities for women and is known as a women's institution. The questionnaire is reprinted below.

QUESTIONNAIRE ON PRISONS FOR
ADULT FEMALES

Name of Prison _____Date_____
General Information
    Average population in this prison in 1970_____
    Approved capacity of this prison_____

Does a felony conviction in this state include the loss of civil rights? _____

If so, may civil rights ever be regained?_____

In California, the common use and availability of drugs is considered to be the greatest contributing factor to the increase of serious crimes by women. Would this be true in your state?_____

If not, what do you consider the greatest influence contributing to the rise of crime among women of your state? _____

Is recidivism a major problem among women parolees in your state?_____

Does this women's prison have the traditional prison wall? _____

Are there any women in this institution under the death sentence _____

If so, how many? _____

Life in Prison

Is there a standard prison dress or uniform?_____

Does this prison have a family visitation program? _____

If so, how often? _____

Are there arrangements for conjugal visitations?

If so, how often? _____

Is there a policy of open correspondence?_____

If not, is mail censored?

       Incoming_____

       Outgoing_____

Is outside 'free world' admitted?

       Religious organizations _____

       High school and/or college teachers_____

       Counselors _____

       Volunteer workers _____

       News media _____

       Entertainers _____

If entertainers are admitted, what type of entertainment would be acceptable? _____

_____

Is there an organized recreational program?____
If so, is it under a trained recreational director?

_____

Is there an 'inmate published' news sheet, magazine or informational letter? _____
Do inmates receive pay for work inside? _____
If so, what jobs receive pay? _____

_____

What is the rate of pay? _____
May prisoners receive money from outside? ____
If so, is there a limitation? _____How
much? _____
Is there a commissary or store to supply personal
needs for inmates? _____
If so, do inmates help staff and/or manage it?
_____Is payment made with
money or some form of scrip? _____

Vocational and Academic Training
Average educational level upon first admittance

_____

Among present prison population, what is the
highest preprison educational level attained?

_____

Is academic training available for inmates?_____
            If so, through what levels? _____
            Elementary _____
            High school _____
            College _____
Are any of the following training programs
offered?
            Nurse's aide _____
            Licensed vocational nurse _____
            Domestic service housekeeping _____
            Sewing (institutional)_____

Hotel, restaurant cooking, baking, cleaning _____

Laundry (institutional or commercial) _____

Business education
   Typing_____
   Shorthand_____
   Keypunch_____
   Business machines_____
   Computer programming____
   Other_____

Medical Facilities Within Prison
   Hospital_____
   Resident doctor_____
   Resident dentist _____
   Psychiatrist _____
   How many babies were born to women prisoners in 1971? _____

Preparation for Release
   Is a work furlough program utilized?_____
   If so, how near her parole date does a woman have this opportunity? _____
   How soon after imprisonment may a woman be released on parole? _____

Parole
   Is there a women's board of parole in your state?
   _____
   If so, how many women serve on it?_____
   Are there any minority members on it?_____
   If there is a women's board of parole, is it made up of political appointees?_____
   What plans are made to assist a released woman?
   Release money_____ How much_____
   Assistance in securing a job _____
   Halfway houses available _____
   Parole supervision
      Close _____
      Very little _____

Other release assistance _____

Prison Staff

Basic training required for administrative positions _____

_____

Are staff members encouraged to undertake in-service training beyond the immediate requirements of their jobs? _____

What training is required for a custody officer (guard)? _____

_____

What is the percentage of male custody officers?

_____

                                   female custody officers?

_____

What   training   is   required   for   counselors?

_____

What is the average counselor load? _____

If the prison employs teachers, are they credentialed under the state education system?_____

_____If not, what

training is required? _____

We learned that some states do not have separate facilities for women; that some have so few women felons that a separate prison would not be justified (Alaska, for example, has an average of 1.2 women felons a year); that conditions vary widely from state to state; and that owing to one factor or another no statistical information on penal life can possibly be considered absolute.

By the time publication was drawing near, a few months had elapsed since the questionnaire had first gone out. To get more recent information, we sent a brief form to all those who had responded to the original questionnaire asking them to comment on and update the data they had supplied.

Some indicated no change. Some, interestingly enough, had already instituted reforms. Indeed, it is not unlikely that still other reforms will have taken place by the time this book has gone to press.

A few wardens did not return the brief form, which left us no choice but to use the statistics from the original questionnaire. We apologize for any inaccuracies resulting from the absence of a response to our second request.

The tables printed here indicate trends; they are not absolute. Some institutions did not answer even the original questionnaire. Standardization of data was difficult, because the terminology used in answering questions varied from institution to institution. Nevertheless, to our knowledge this is the first time even this much information has been compiled in a form available to the general public. This work is offered as a beginning, with the hope that penology specialists will produce more complete information for the tax-paying public about women's prisons nationally and the possibilities for reform.

In considering reform it is important to remember that the type of woman prisoner is changing. The increased tendency to put certain convicts on probation or into work release programs may indicate that those who *are* incarcerated are women with a long history of crime. Such women may be less likely to respond to rehabilitation programs. The rise in drug usage has also brought into crime a type of woman never before associated with it.

While it is much more expensive to keep a woman in prison than in a good halfway house or work release program or on probation, the cost in terms of money is not the only measure. There are strong humanitarian reasons for avoiding total incarceration. Approximately

90 percent-plus of the convicts in prison today can and will respond to rehabilitation. To truly rehabilitate them and at the same time protect society against the 5 to 10 percent who consistently fail to react well to any positive program is the real challenge.

Effective solutions cannot be found by any one group or segment of society. The solution will have to come from all of us. It is to the advantage of the general public to initiate and support programs which will help a woman felon become a self-respecting, contributing member of society.

1

GENERAL INFORMATION

State	Approved Capacity	Number of Inmates 1971-72	Ages of Inmates	Loss of Civil Rights	Civil Rights Regained	Recidivism	Prison Wall	Standard Dress	Family Friends Visit	Conjugal Visits	Other Information
Alabama	350	125	18-68	Yes	After pardon	Less than 20%	Cyclone fence	Yes	Yes weekly	No	
California	900	590	18+	Yes	Yes	37%—5% new charge	Barbed wire on roof	May wear own clothes	At certain hrs.	Yes*	*6 mos. after imprisonment, on good behavior
Colorado	90	75-80	16+	Yes	Yes	9%	No wall	No	Saturday & Sunday	*	*On earned leaves *On emergency leaves
Connecticut	232	180	16+	Yes	Yes	A problem	No wall	No	4 per month	No	
Delaware	40	25	18+	NA	NA	Yes*	No wall	Yes	Holidays	No	*Institution estimates 70%
Georgia	150	260	16+	Yes	Yes	19%	No wall	Yes	Saturday & Sunday	No	
Illinois	220	107.3	17+	May vote when released*	Yes	9.9%	No wall	May wear own clothes	Once a week	No	*Lost during incarceration, regained when released from parole supervision
Indiana	160	142	18+	No	NA	Misdemeanors 29¾%*	No wall	No	1 hr. every 2 wks.	No	*Felons, 8½% Parole violat. 11%+
Iowa	80	65-70	18+	Yes	Yes	Less than 15%	No wall or fence	No	Every day	No*	*Has home furlough plan
Kansas	100	63.3	16+	Yes	Yes	No problem	No wall	No	Every 2 wks.*	No	*For 2 hours
Kentucky	93	105	16+	Yes	Yes	14%	Fence	No	One per week*	No	*Per family member or approved visitor
Maine	60	30	16+	No	NA	No problem	No wall	No	1 each week	No	
Maryland	225	120	16+	No	NA	23%	Fence	No	1 each week	No	
Massachusetts	200	152	None	Yes	Yes	Less than 30%	No wall	No	1 hr. per week	No	
Minnesota	70	55	18+	Yes	When discharged	28%	No wall	No	4 per month	No*	*Home furlough up to 5 days
Missouri	80	90+	17+	Yes	Yes	40%	No wall	No	4 per mo.	No	

Nebraska	73	50	15+	Yes	Yes	15%	Fence	No	Yes		
Nevada	40	33	18+	Yes	Apply to pardon bd.	No problem	No wall	No	Yes	No	
New Jersey	298	230	16+	Yes	Yes	No problem	No wall	Yes	1 per week	No	
New York	430	275	16+	Yes	Yes	No problem	No wall	No	Yes	Yes*	Through home furlough*
North Carolina	488	335	16+	Yes	Yes	No problem	No wall	Yes	1 per week	No	
Ohio	400	300	16+	Yes	Yes	No problem	No wall	Yes	Yes	No	
Oregon	In process of establishing separate facilities for women										
Pennsylvania	300	150	16+	No	NA	A problem	No wall or fence	No	Yes, daily	No	
Rhode Island	Women's reformatory closed										
South Carolina	116	143	17	Yes	Yes	No problem	No wall	Yes	Weekly	No	
Tennessee	100	136	18+	Yes	Yes*	15%	Fence and wire	Has choice	Daily visits	No	Through court after release*
Texas	500	536	18+	Yes	Apply to bd. of pardon and parole	No problem	No wall	Yes	Yes*	No	**2 adults every 2 weeks. Children no limit
Virginia	359	230	17-88	Yes	Yes	No problem	No wall	Yes	Every 2 weeks	No	
West Virginia	60	22	16+	Yes	After parole	No problem	No wall	No	1 day per week	No	
Washington	178	140	18+ *	Yes	Yes	3%	No wall	No	Saturday or Sunday	**	*Judge may recommend 16 yr. old **Furlough system
Wisconsin	161	135	18+	Yes	Yes	13%	No wall	No	Every day	No	

Key: NA—no answer given
*—see Other Information column

Note: In states having no special facilities for women, contract arrangements have been made with other states, as follows:
1. Idaho with Oregon.
2. Hawaii with California.
3. Montana, North Dakota, South Dakota, and Wyoming with Nebraska.
4. Michigan houses its female felony commitments in the Detroit House of Correction.
States not listed in any category have facilities near the men's facilities or cooperating with them.
Florida appears to have a fine program going, with a woman warden in charge of both men's and women's facilities.

General Information—Summary

Few prisons for women appear to be filled to their approved capacity. This is not to be taken as evidence that crime is decreasing among women; in fact, the last decade has shown a sharp increase.

However, there has also been a greater tendency to release women on probation if at all possible. In addition, other facilities are available for first offenders in many states, as are rehabilitation centers for the treatment of drug addicts.

Most states report loss of civil rights upon conviction of felony, but they also provide ways to regain some of those rights upon completion of parole. Usually application must be made through the governor's office. In California a woman who is granted a Gold Seal pardon also regains her civil rights.

Whether or not recidivism is a problem seems to be a matter of judgment. Only seventeen states gave firm answers on this, but it would seem that a state with more than 15 percent recidivism has a problem. Some women are returned to prison because of breaking parole rules. Others become involved in new crime and return with additional commitments.

High walls around women's prisons seem to be nonexistent, though a few (six) state that fences are used, cyclone or barbed wire.

Twenty-one institutions have abandoned the old prison uniform. Nine still insist on some kind of standard dress. Some allow women to choose between the institution uniform and their own clothes. There is a growing tendency toward relaxing dress codes.

All prisons give visiting privileges to family and friends, but the visitors must be approved by administrative staff. Rules vary from very complicated and restrictive to considerably flexible.

So far only one prison, California Institution for Women, has a private apartment on the grounds suitable for conjugal visits. Six prisons reported the liberal use of a home furlough policy as a means for private family visits. Such furloughs are granted only after a specified period of good behavior.

2

STAFF EDUCATION REQUIREMENTS

State	Administrative	Custody Officer	Number or % Female-Male	Counselors	Average Load	Teachers	Other Information
Alabama	Equivalent to college grad	H. S.	81% F	M.A. in related fields*	126	State Credential	*Work experience
California	B.A. degree and related experience	H.S. grad. or GED for males* 60 coll. units for females	90% F	College degree**	120	State Credential	*In-service training **Group counseling experience
Colorado	Six yrs. experience in admin. or college degree*	Ongoing in-service training	35 F, 1 M	Experience or college	30	State Credential	*Ongoing in-service training
Connecticut	M.A. + 3 weeks Training Academy	3 weeks Training Academy	65 F, 12 M	Bachelor of Science*	40	State Credential	*One week Training Academy
Delaware	In-service training	In-service training	10 F	Have none*	NA	State Credential	*2 outside counselors on call
Georgia	College degree	H.S.	42 total	M.A. plus experience	60	State Credential	
Illinois	Depends on position	Prefers H.S. grad.	49 F	B.A.	50 to 100	State Credential	
Indiana	College degree + experience in field	H.S.	35, all F	4 yrs. college	75*	State Credential	*Has 2 counselors
Iowa	B.A. or M.A.	H.S. plus	2 M	Staff team Structure	Does not apply	State Credential*	*Uses teachers from local schools, community college Contracts on hourly basis.
Kansas	College degree*	120 hrs. + 4 to 6 weeks on job**	97.1% F 2.9% M	1 classification officer	69	State Credential	*Major in sociol. & psychology Admin. exper. in penal instit. **40 hrs. behavioral science
Kentucky	Degree in penology	H.S. + some college	16 F, 6 M	M.S.W. degree*	35 to 50	State Credential	*Master Social Work, has 1 counselor
Maine	Experience most important	No minimum given	80% F 20% M	NA	NA	State Credential	
Maryland	Work experience or academic	Varies	90% F 10% M	Bachelor of Science	20	College degree	
Massachusetts	Experience most important	In-service only	43 F, 6 M	B.A. or M.A.	30	State Credential	
Minnesota	M.A. in social work	H.S. minimum*	26 F, 3 M	B.A. or M.A.	25	State Credentail	*Special correspondence courses; must attend Academy

	College degree + experience*	Civil Service test	90% F 10% M	Civil Service test		State Credential**	
Missouri	College degree + experience*	Civil Service test	90% F 10% M	Civil Service test	90	State Credential	*In academic & vocational **Teachers must have experience in Corrections.
Nebraska	H.S. + much experience	On-job training	85% F	No professional counselors*	NA	State Credential	*Pastoral counseling on request Volunteers from community Group therapy with teacher
Nevada	Varies*	H.S. + two years work experience	13 F, 2 M	4 yrs. coll. + 1 yr. exper.	33	State Credential	*Usually college degree
New Jersey	M.A. in social work	H.S. or equivalent	83 F, 1 M**	B.A. or M.A.*	20	State Credential	*B.A. in sociol. or psych. or M.A. in social work or related fields **Also 7 male correction officers
New York	Civil service in all positions		159 F, 15 M	Civil Service	100	State Credential	
North Carolina	Basic training*	Two weeks**	80% F	M.A. social work	100	State Credential	*No details given **In Custody and Human Relations
Ohio	College + experience	Civil Service	76 F, 19 M	Bachelor of Science*	35 to 40	State Credential	*Minimum
Pennsylvania	Nine weeks training*	H.S. + 9 weeks training*	75 F, 15 M	B.S. degree + 9 weeks training*	50	State Credential	*3 weeks at bureau level 6 weeks at institution
Rhode Island	Women's Reformatory closed						
South Carolina	B.A. degree	H.S. + in-service	24 F, 10 M	Bachelor of Science	20	State Credential	
Tennessee	M.A. for warden	H.S. + two weeks special training	20 F, 19 M	Degree in social work*	35 to 50	State Credential	*Or related field
Texas	No set criteria	H.S. + in-service	46 F, 8 M	Bachelor of Science	37*	State Credential	*In group counseling, also has individual sessions
Virginia	College degree	4 weeks orientation training	50% F	Bachelor of Science	50 to 75	State Credential	
West Virginia	Depends on position	In-service training	8 F, 4 M	Has none		State Credential	
Washington	B.A. + 4 yrs. admin. experience	*		2 yrs. exp.** 2 yrs. college	32	State Credential	*Custody officer—see Summary **Experience must be in Corrections
Wisconsin	M.A. in social work	H.S. or equivalent*	95% F	B.S. and Master's	35 to 40	State Credential	+Continued ongoing training

Key: NA—no answer given
*—see Other Information column

Staff Education Requirements—Summary

Most states appear to have relatively high training requirements for staff at administrative level.
In general this is true of counselors.

Teacher training requirements adhere to state
credential systems. However, this does not tell the
whole story. In California the credential requirements are high—a four-year college degree plus one
year which includes practice teaching at various
levels. In other states the requirements are lower,
with many differences between high and low
standards.

There appears to be noticeable weakness in training requirements for custody officers, with a few
states having no basic requirements while others
have only in-service training.

The Purdy Treatment Center for Women (Gig
Harbor, Washington) uses a system of living units,
with thirty-two women and a counselor per unit.
The women go from the 'intake unit' through the
various units, each carrying more personal responsibility, progressing toward the outlet or 'exit unit,'
her final step toward freedom.

The plan is too detailed to explain in a book of
this kind, but it has shown some very promising results. In its two years of operation, recidivism
among women has been cut from 12 percent to 3
percent; the average length of stay has been cut
from eighteen months to sixteen months.

The custodial role of the cottage counselors is not
emphasized. Ideally they present an image to the
prisoners that says: "You are worth trying to help.
Other people do care about you."

Since there is daily contact between inmate and

staff, it would seem that importance should be placed on recruiting individuals with a good basic education plus a high potential for work with prisoners. Perhaps this area should be examined by all the states, including a survey of salaries offered in positions of this nature.

MEDICAL FACILITIES[3]

State	Hospital on Premises	Resident Doctor	Dentist	Psychiatrist	Babies Born 1971-72	Other Information
Alabama	Yes	Dr. comes daily & on call	Weekly & on call	Weekly, by appointment	6	
California	Yes	Yes, 3	Yes, 2	Yes, 1	25	
Colorado	Yes	Yes	Yes	Yes	6*	*Outside hospital
Connecticut	Yes	Yes, 3	1, part-time	2, part-time	18	
Delaware	No*	Yes	Clinic outside	As needed	2**	*Uses local hospital **Outside hospital
Georgia	No	Part-time	No	Part-time	5	
Illinois	Yes	2 days each week and on 24 hr. call	Two days a week	Part-time	3	
Indiana	Yes	Contractual, part-time	Contractual, part-time	On emergency or contract	8*	*At Indiana University Medical Center, as0 prenatal and postnatal care
Iowa	Infirmary	Contractual, 1 visit per week	Contractual	Half-day per week	8*	*Outside hospital
Kansas	Yes	On call	On call	By request*	7	*If court recommends
Kentucky	Yes	2, part-time	Part-time	Part-time	9	Has registered nurse (RN)
Maine	No*	Part-time	Part-time	Part-time	NA	*Uses local hospital
Maryland	Dispensary	3 consulting	1 consulting	1 consulting	6 to 10*	*Yearly average
Massachusetts	Yes	Part-time	Part-time	Half-day per week	8	
Minnesota	No	2 half-days per week	Half-day bi-weekly	Half-day every 2 weeks	2	

State	Infirmary						Other Information
Missouri						2	=Regional centers used when needed
Nebraska	No, but has RN	On call	No	No	No	3	
Nevada	No*	Yes**	Yes**	Yes**	*	1	*Uses local hospital **Shares with men's facilities
New Jersey	Yes	Part-time	Full-time	Full-time	2 days per week	10 in 1972	
New York	Yes	Yes	Yes	Yes	Part-time on call*	6	=Full-time psychologist
North Carolina	Clinic service	NA	NA	NA	Yes	17	
Ohio	Yes	Part-time	Part-time	Part-time	Full-time	9	
Oregon	In process of establishing separate facilities for women						
Pennsylvania	Yes	Part-time	Part-time	Part-time	Part-time	8	
Rhode Island	Women's Reformatory closed						
South Carolina	No*	*	*	*	*	2	=Uses Dept. of Corrections medical facilities
Tennessee	Clinic; full-time RN	Half-day per week	Half-day per week*	No	No	11	*Also has volunteer dental service
Texas	Yes	Yes	Yes	Yes	Yes	20	
Virginia	Clinic	Part-time	Part-time	Part-time	Part-time	21	
West Virginia	No	Part-time, once a week	NA	NA	NA	2	
Washington	Clinic	Part-time	Part-time	Part-time	Part-time	0	
Wisconsin	Yes	One-half time	Yes	Yes	Yes	NA	

Key: NA—no answer given
*—see Other Information column

Medical Facilities—Summary

States which have a full-time doctor, dentist, and psychiatrist, plus a hospital inside or on the grounds, are probably giving the inmates all the care necessary. Although the questionnaire did not cover the work of volunteer medical people, many institutions do have them available.

Those without full-time medical people are endeavoring to meet their needs as best they can with limited budgets. The survey reveals a number of probable weak areas.

Another problem unique in prisons for women is the birth of babies. Last year 228 or more (some did not report) babies were born to inmates. This means that the institution must concern itself not only with infant health needs but also with foster home placement, adoption procedures, or release to the woman's family.

Because so many women who find themselves in prison are in their twenty's and early thirty's, the baby problem will continue. Increased knowledge and the use of dependable contraceptives may lower the birth rate. One should keep in mind, however, that most individuals who have reached a felon's prison have never had a high degree of self-discipline. Nor have they felt a deep sense of responsibility for the results of their own actions.

In very progressive prisons for women an inmate may receive as much or more medical care than she did in her old environment. California Institution for Women can point to many cases of corrective work done to remove or reduce deformities or crippling conditions which were and would continue to be a serious obstacle to successful life in a competitive society. But *that* road is not recommended as a means of getting medical care! There are better ways to come by it in the world outside.

4

CONTACT WITH FREE WORLD

State	Open Correspondence*	Mail Opened	Mail Censored	Free World Admitted	Inmate Newspaper	Organized Recreation	Other Information *Inmate may correspond with anyone she pleases
Alabama	On approval	Yes	Yes	On approval	Yes	No	
California	On approval	Yes*	No*	Yes, clubs, college classes, entertainers	Yes	Yes, with director	*Legal outgoing to attorneys and officials not opened. 10% incoming examined for contraband
Colorado	No	Read	Read	Yes*	No	Yes	*Limit on news media
Connecticut	Restricted list	Examined for contraband	No	Yes	Yes	Yes*	*No director
Delaware	No	Incoming yes Outgoing no		Yes	No*	Yes	*Opportunity to start paper is available. May contribute articles to men's news bulletin.
Georgia	Approved list	Sometimes	Sometimes	Yes	No	Yes	
Illinois	Limited*	Incoming*	Outgoing*	Yes: visiting groups, volunteers	Yes, not regular	Yes, no director	*May receive mail from anyone but write only to those on approved list. Incoming mail checked for contraband. Outgoing spot-checked. Incoming read but not censored
Indiana	Limited	Yes	Yes	Yes	No	Yes*	*With director and recreation aide
Iowa		Incoming spotchecked*	No	Yes	No	No	*May be examined for money
Kansas	NA	Incoming*		Yes	No	Yes**	*Soon to be uncensored **No director in summer
Kentucky	Yes	Yes	No	Yes	Yes	Yes	
Maine	NA	Incoming		Yes	No	Yes, no director	
Maryland	NA	Yes	No	Yes	Yes	Yes	
Massachusetts	NA	Yes	No	Yes	Yes*	Yes	*Inmate paper 3 or 4 times a year; censored by administration

							Other Information
Minnesota	Yes	Yes	*	Yes**	Yes	Yes	*Censored only for security women **150 volunteers come in and work with women
Missouri	Yes	Yes	No	Yes	No	*	*In planning stage
Nebraska	No	Yes	Yes	Yes*	No	No	*News media as advised
Nevada	*	NA	No	Yes	No	No	*Approved list
New Jersey	Yes	Yes	No	Yes	No	Yes	
New York	NA	No	Yes*	Yes	Yes	Yes	*Censorship is liberal
North Carolina	Yes	Incoming		Yes	Underway	Yes	
Ohio	Yes	Yes	No	Yes	Yes	Yes	
Oregon	In process of establishing separate facilities for women						
Pennsylvania	Yes	NA	NA	Yes*	No**	Soon will have	*Free world contact encouraged **Resident Advisory Council gives information to peers; serves as newspaper
Rhode Island	Women's Reformatory closed						
South Carolina	Yes	Yes	No	Yes	Yes	Yes	
Tennessee	Yes	No	No	Yes	Yes	Yes	
Texas	Outgoing yes Incoming no	Incoming	No	Yes*	Yes	Yes	*Volunteers help with women
Virginia	No*	NA	NA	Yes	Yes	Yes	*Except to attorneys, public officials
West Virginia	No	Yes	Yes	Yes	No	No	
Washington	NA	Yes	NA	Yes	Yes	Yes	
Wisconsin	NA	Yes	No	Yes	No*	Yes	*Not now. Failed, may try again

Key: NA—no answer given
  *—see Other Information column

Contact with Free World—Summary

All prisons seem to have increasing contact with the "free world," through visiting classes, service clubs and entertainment. This does not mean a continual 'open house'; security reasons alone would prevent this. Also, loss of mobility, the freedom to come and go as one pleases, to see friends of one's own choice, are what prison is all about. Prison administrations vary in their attitudes toward admission of people from outside. A bad experience or two in the state generally causes a tightening up in all the penal institutions.

There is a general movement now toward allowing more contact with the outside as a means of helping inmates to keep aware of the fact that 'there's a world out there,' and that one day most of them will return to it. Also, this inside-outside contact means a better informed public, who presumably will see the areas of weakness and be more willing to support reform measures. Some wardens are very strict about the types of outside activity coming in; others are more lenient. Music groups are always welcome.

There has been some confusion as to the meaning of open correspondence. Actually, this means that an inmate may correspond with anyone she pleases as often as she pleases. However, most institutions require some kind of screening before a name goes on a resident's list for correspondence approval. Mail is not actually censored in many prisons, but often the incoming mail is spot-checked for contraband such as money or drugs. Indiana states that the entire Department of Corrections is working on new regulations for correspondence and, for better plans for admitting books and magazines more freely.

Newspapers published by residents are growing in popularity. Censorship varies according to the general policies of the institution.

Recreation programs seem to be very general in most prisons. Volunteer workers from outside often help. Some prisons have a recreation director on the staff; many more do not.

5

EDUCATION AVAILABLE

State	Aver. on Admittance	Highest on Admittance	Available in Prison	Typing	Short-hand	Key punch	Business Machines	Other Information
Alabama	Gr. 8.6	2 yrs. jr. college	Grades, H.S., & GED*	Being considered	No	Being considered	Being considered	*General education diploma
California	Gr. 8.3	M.A.	Grades, H.S., college classes*	Yes	Yes	Yes	Yes	
Colorado	Gr. 9.8	B.A.	Gr. 6, GED, college classes*	Yes	Yes	No	No	*By extension Bookkeeping, filing, office procedures also available
Connecticut	Gr. 8	3 yrs. college	H.S. some college	Yes	Yes	Yes	Yes	Computer
Delaware	Gr. 8	3 yrs. college	Grades, H.S., some college	Yes	Yes	*	*	*To be offered in new programs. Also computer programming
Georgia	Gr. 6	College graduate	Grades, H.S., college*	Yes	Yes	Yes	Yes	*Educational Release Program
Illinois	Gr. 9	2 yrs. college	Lower elementary to A.A.* degree	Yes	Yes	Yes	Yes	*Associate of Arts
Indiana	Gr. 9	College graduate	Grades, H.S., college*	Yes	Yes	No	Yes	*College by correspondence Beauty school
Iowa	Gr. 9	College graduate	Grades, GED, Learning Lab, college*	Yes	As needed	As needed	As needed	*College at Iowa Central Community College, Ft. Dodge
Kansas	Gr. 9	College graduate	Grades, H.S., college*	Yes	Yes	**	Special	*College by correspondence **Available in Leavenworth + computer 24-week course MOTA business machines, clerk training
Kentucky	Gr. 6	College graduates	Grades through H.S.	Yes	Yes	Yes		
Maine	Gr. 9	Gr. 12	Grades through H.S.	Yes	No	No	No	
Maryland	Gr. 5 to 6	Gr. 12	Grades through H.S.	Yes	No	No	No	
Massachusetts	Gr. 10	1 yr. college	Grades through H.S. or equivalent	Yes	NA	NA	*	*Being installed
Minnesota	Gr. 10*	2 yrs. college	Grades through H.S.**	Yes	Yes	Yes	Yes	*60% are 12th gr. or GED **H.S. and some college by correspondence Bookkeeping now available

			Grades through H.S.*					*Coaching for GED
Missouri	Gr. 9	2 yrs. college	Grades through H.S.*	Yes	Yes	Yes	NA	
Nebraska	Gr. 10	2 yrs. college	Grades through H.S.	Yes	Yes	NA	NA	
Nevada	Gr. 9.5	B.A.	Grades through H.S. college*	Yes	Yes	Yes	Yes**	*College by correspondence **Computer programming
New Jersey	Gr. 8	B.A.	H.S., college courses	Yes	Yes	Yes	Yes	
New York	Gr. 6	College graduate	Grades through H.S., college*	Yes	Yes	Yes	NA	*Community college
North Carolina	Gr. 8	NA	Grades through H.S., jr. college	Yes	Yes	Yes	Yes	
Ohio	Gr. 9	Attorney	Grades through H.S., college*	Yes	Yes	Yes	Yes	*College by correspondence Computer
Oregon	In process of establishing separate facilities for women							
Pennsylvania	NA	College graduate	Grades through H.S.	Yes	Yes	Yes	NA	
Rhode Island	Closed							
South Carolina	Gr. 8	2 yrs. college	Grades through H.S.	Yes	Speed Writing	No	NA	Through Community Resources Program, any training may be requested in community facilities
Tennessee	Gr. 5.1	3 yrs. college	Grades, H.S. GED, college	Yes	Yes	No	No	Receptionist, staff aide training
Texas	Gr. 6.3	M.A.	Grades through college	Yes	Yes	Yes	Yes	
Virginia	Gr. 8	College graduate	Grades through H.S., college courses	Yes	NA	NA	Yes	Filing & records
West Virginia	Gr. 8	Gr. 12	Grades through H.S.	Yes	Yes*	Yes*	Yes	*After Jan. 1, 1972, filing and records
Washington	Gr. 10	M.A.	Grades through H.S., A.A.*	Yes	Yes	Yes	Yes	*Associate of Arts degree in community college Computer
Wisconsin	Gr. 9.5	College graduate	Grades through H.S.	Yes	Yes	Yes	Yes	Computer

Key: NA—no answer given
*—see Other Information column

Education Available—Summary

The school grade level the new resident gives on admittance is often not valid. She does not want to reveal that she dropped out of school at 6th grade or lower. Testing in the institution usually suggests a grade or more under.

Whether the statement of the inmate or that of the institution is accepted, educational levels range wide, from almost total illiteracy to a master's degree.

Although many of these women may have been grade school drop-outs, in other ways they are adult women of varying intelligence and with various kinds of problems.

This wide disparity in educational levels at admittance makes it very difficult to meet all needs inside. Elementary and high school subjects can be handled at most institutions, but college courses are not usually available.

If a woman is on minimum custody she may be allowed to take courses at a local community college. This program seems to be meeting with increasing approval and success. Or a resident may take college courses by correspondence if she has money to pay for them.

For those who may have a good background of general knowledge and the determination to strengthen their weak areas, most prisons provide coaching for the general education diploma. With a GED the inmate can enroll in college-level courses.

Self-motivation is another problem. People in prison usually have little hope that more education will be helpful in their situation. Several prisons have or are working on programs to encourage residents to make greater efforts to use their time toward self-improvement.

State	Nurse's Aide	Licensed Vocational Nurse	Domestic Service	Sewing	Hotel Baking, Cleaning	Laundry	Other Information
Alabama	No	No	No	Yes	No	Yes	Cosmetology, floral design
California	Yes	Yes	Yes	Yes	Yes	No	IBM word processing (MT/ST), cosmetology, pattern making & grading, manicurist, wiggery (licensure program)
Colorado	No	No	No	Yes	Yes	Yes	Janitorial service, food services
Connecticut	Yes	NA	Yes	Yes	Yes	Yes	
Delaware	Yes—outside	Yes	Yes	Yes	Only as institutional work		
Georgia	Yes	No	Yes	Yes*	NA	Yes	*Institutional sewing, kitchen training
Illinois	No	Being planned*	Being planned*	Yes	On job	Yes	*All programs being improved
Indiana	In plan	No	No	Yes*	No	Yes	*Institutional sewing Beauty school, business courses, 5 go out on vocational release
Iowa	Yes	Yes	On job	Yes	Yes	Yes	Advanced tailoring
Kansas	Yes	*	On job	Yes	On job	Yes	*Available in Leavenworth
Kentucky	Yes	Yes	Yes	Yes	Yes	Yes	Supermarket checkout, upholstery (Jan. 1973)
Maine	Yes	No	Yes	Yes	Yes	Yes	
Maryland	No	No	No	Yes	On work release	Yes	
Massachusetts	NA	NA	On job	On job	Yes	Yes	
Minnesota	No	No	No	Yes	No	Yes	Food service program, Sauk Centre program

State							Cosmetology—can be licensed
Missouri	Yes	No	No	On job	Yes	Yes	
Nebraska	NA	NA	NA	Yes	Yes*	NA	*Hotel rehabilitation program / Beginning vocational rehabilitation programs
Nevada	No	NA	NA	Yes*	Yes	Yes	*Institutional sewing
New Jersey	Yes	No	Yes	Yes	Yes	Yes	Beauty culture, electronics assembly
New York	No	No	Yes	Yes	Yes	Yes	Beauty culture
North Carolina	Yes	No	NA	Yes	Yes	Yes	
Ohio	On job	No	Yes	Yes	Yes	Yes	
Oregon		Programs too new to report					
Pennsylvania	Yes	NA	NA	Yes	NA	Yes	
Rhode Island	Women's State Reformatory has closed						
South Carolina	Yes	Yes	Yes	Yes	Yes	Yes	Any vocation requested if it is available in the community
Tennessee	On job*	On job*	On job*	Yes	Yes	No	*Only on work details / Cosmetology, dental technician added
Texas	Yes	Yes	Yes	Yes	Yes	Yes	Cosmetology, floristry, horticulture
Virginia	NA	NA	On job	Yes	On job	On job	Cosmetology, business
West Virginia	NA	NA	NA	NA	NA	Yes	West Virginia planned to expand the vocational training after Jan. 1972. / No reply to follow-up questionnaire
Washington	No	No	No	No	Yes	No	
Wisconsin	Yes	No	Yes	Yes	Yes	Yes	

Key: NA—no answer given
   *—see Other Information column

Vocational Training—Summary

Although vocational programs have too often in the past been the day labor of prisons, the winds of change are rising in these areas.

Laundry is still considered part of the vocational training program in many institutions, but some no longer list it as such. Other prisons will no doubt follow as money is made available to meet this very necessary part of institutional maintenance.

Several prison wardens have written that new vocational programs are to begin soon or that they are in the stage of planning.

Many states hesitate to offer vocational nursing (LVN) programs because of drug temptation. Nurse's aide programs are more acceptable.

Indiana allows certain women to go off campus daily for training in library science and accounting. Five are now doing this, with hopes that five or six more will soon be involved in nurse's aide training off campus.

South Carolina also offers flexibility of choice of vocational training. Women are allowed to train for any vocation offered in the community. This privilege probably involves a limited number, because only the women who can handle that much freedom are permitted off campus.

Iowa sends this information: "We are moving into a program of contracting with clients as part of the Education-Treatment design. This is compatible with Achievement Motivation and directly related to it. It will provide specific information to staff and clients for measurable specific performance. When all phases of contracts are completed the client will be released to work release or parole. The time element will be contingent upon client activity and level of achievement."

Minnesota has also launched an off-grounds vocational program. A food services program is also proving quite successful. If a woman remains in this program for a year, she will be able to obtain a certificate qualifying her for a food manager-type job upon release. During the program she is trained in all kinds of food preparation, budget preparation, etc.

In Minnesota The Sauk Centre Program is proving successful. In 1972 four women were granted conditional paroles and placed at the Minnesota Home School at Sauk Centre (state juvenile institution) as teacher's aides and as counselors for the residents. Actually, these women are serving their incarceration by learning a job skill that should increase their employability upon discharge.

The more progressive institutions seem to be moving toward using community-based training and/or educational programs wherever possible. If this is generally successful the financial burden should be measurably lessened.

Discussion with several women on parole has revealed agreement that prisoners should be required to do all institutional work as part of their payment to society. They add emphatically, however, that they do not want it called training! They want it called what it is . . . institutional labor. They are willing to give several hours a day to the institution, if they can have time for real training programs. "Don't tell us that mopping that dining room floor, washing windows etc., is vocational training. No way!"

State	Pay for Work Inside	Money from Outside	Limit on Spending	Store	Money Used	Inmate Help in Prison Store	Other Information
Alabama	No.* All receive 50c per week allowance	Yes	$15 per week	Yes	Money	With stock only	*Person operating snack bar is paid
California	5c to 19c per hour $7.50 to $16.50 per month	Yes	$40 per month	Yes	Scrip	Yes	
Colorado	15c to 75c per day	Yes	$50 per month	Yes	Plastic	Yes	
Connecticut	24c to 74c per day	Yes	NA	Yes	Money	Yes	
Delaware	$4 to $8 per month	Yes	$65 per month	Yes	Commissary card	Yes	
Georgia	*	Yes	None	Yes	Money	Yes	*Only those on vocational rehabilitation, on certain jobs
Illinois	Industry to $45 per month; others $4 to $7 per month	Yes	$10 per week*	Yes	Account system	Yes	*No spending limits on honor unit residents
Indiana	$2 to $6 per month	Yes, $25 at a time; kept in trust account	$10 per week for commissary	Yes*	Punch card system	Yes**	*No clothing **Assigned to staff responsible for commissary
Iowa	15c to 30c per hour; max. $2.40 per day*	Yes, no limit	No	Yes	Money	Yes	*Except for authorized overtime
Kansas	5c to 30c per day	Yes, no limit	NA	Yes	NA	NA	
Kentucky	12c per day	Yes	$10 per week	Yes	Canteen card	Yes	
Maine	No	Yes, no limit	NA	Yes	Money	Yes	
Maryland	40c to $1 per day	Yes	NA	Yes	Coupons	Yes	
Massachusetts	35c to 50c per day	Yes, no limit	NA	Yes	Store card	Yes	
Minnesota	95c per day maximum	Yes, no limit	No	*	Money	Yes	*Special ordering days from local store

State							Other Information
Missouri	$3 per month	Yes	NA	Yes	Scrip	Yes	
Nebraska	25¢ to 50¢ per day	Yes, no limit	NA	Yes	Scrip	Yes	*$3 minimum, $22.50 maximum per month
Nevada	Yes, mostly clerical jobs*	Yes, no limit	$15 per week	No			
New Jersey	65¢ to $1 per day	Yes, no limit	NA	Yes	Institutional account	Yes	
New York	25¢ to $1 per day	Yes, no limit	NA	Yes	Scrip	Yes	
North Carolina	No	Yes, to $10 per week	NA	Yes	Money	Yes	
Ohio	10¢ per hour	Yes	NA	Yes	Book account	Yes	
Oregon	Newly established separate facilities. No policies or procedures available						
Pennsylvania	50¢ to $1 per day	Yes	NA	Yes	Charge account	Yes	
Rhode Island	Women's Reformatory closed						
South Carolina	$14 to $21 per month	Yes	No	Yes	Chips	Yes	*Coins given for Coke machine
Tennessee	$6 to $13 per month	Yes	Up to $25 twice a month	Yes	Tickets*	No	
Texas	No	Yes	Yes	Yes	Scrip	Yes	
Virginia	25¢ per day*	Yes	NA	Yes	Tickets	Yes	*10¢ to 50¢ bonus per day
West Virginia	10¢ per working day	Yes	NA	Yes	Vouchers	No	
Washington	25¢ to 30¢ per hour	Yes	NA	Yes	Special checkbook	Yes	
Wisconsin	50¢ per day	Yes	$7.50 per week	Yes	NA	No	May order from catalogue with approval; no limits

Key: NA—no answer given
*—see Other Information column

Money in Prison—Summary

At first thought it would seem that no prison inmate should need money. However, this is not true. Certain personal needs remain, such as personal grooming supplies. And nearly all the women smoke. "There's nothing else to do!" they will often say. Some residents can earn a limited amount by making and selling various handwork through the prison store or office, if such an outlet is available.

Policies of paying for work done in prison vary greatly. North Carolina, Texas and Maine pay nothing, while in Iowa a resident may earn as much as $2.40 per day, with the possibility of overtime. Residents who are paid the most usually have come to prison with certain skills. This is particularly true of clerical jobs.

Some institutions put no limit on amount of money an inmate may receive from outside but do regulate the amount she may spend. Thus women are encouraged to build up their account funds to use when released. Just as in the world outside, a few can save even from very meager sums; others wouldn't save a penny without some control on inside spending.

Only a few prisons allow the women to have real money in their quarters. Anything that is negotiable outside adds to the temptation to try to escape. Some wardens, however, feel that inmates should be allowed possession of money as part of the rehabilitation training.

State	Women's Parole Board	Women on Parole Board	Minority Members	How Appointed	Work Release	Release Money	Half-way House	Job Assistance	Other Information
Alabama	No	NA	NA	By governor	Yes	$10 + bus fare	No	Parole officer, counselor, family	
California	Yes	3	No	By governor	Yes	$68*	Yes	Parole officer, vocational rehabilitation, Trade Advisory Committees	*If convict's assets are under $200
Colorado	No	No	Yes	Civil Service	No	$100	Yes	Parolees given clothing, counseling*	*Assigned to volunteers and to professionals
Connecticut	No	1	Yes	NA	Yes	Yes	No	No set policy, each case treated individually	
Delaware	No	2	2	By governor	Yes	No	No	"Give all assistance we can"	
Georgia	No	No	No	By governor	Yes	$25	Yes	Labor Department vocational rehabilitation	
Illinois	No	1	4 of 10	By governor	Yes	$50	Yes*	Outside agencies helpful	*In Chicago and St. Louis
Indiana	Yes	4	2	Political appointment	Yes*	Varies	None	Parole officers, counselors, community volunteers**	*Also educational release **When available
Iowa	No	0	Yes	Political appointment	Yes	To $100	Yes	Prerelease counseling by parole officers and others	
Kansas	No	0*	1	NA	No	$25 + bus fare	NA	Parole officer, vocational rehabilitation	*3 men on parole board
Kentucky	No	1	1	By governor	No	$35	1	Prerelease counseling	
Maine	Yes	1	No	By commissioner	Yes	On need	Yes	Parole officer	
Maryland	No	0	Yes	Political appointment	Yes	$20 min.	Yes	Parole officer, family, community	
Massachusetts	No	1	1	NA	Yes	$50	Yes	Parole officer, others	
Minnesota	No	1	2	By governor	Yes	$100	*	Parole officer, social workers, volunteers	*Being planned
Missouri	No	No*	NA	NA	**	$25 + bus fare	2	Vocational rehabilitation	*Female parole officers act as parole board **Just beginning work release

State								Assistance	Other Information
Nebraska	No	NA	No	NA	Yes	Yes, no set am't	Yes*	Assistance given; no specific plan	*1 in Omaha, 1 in Lincoln
Nevada	No	1	No	By governor	Yes	$25	No	Assistance given, no details	
New York	No	NA	NA	NA	Yes	$40	Yes	Institutional or employment parole officer*	*Available community agencies
New Jersey	No	0*	Yes	Not political	Yes	$50 maximum	Yes	Assistance given; no details	*No women on state board of parole. Men and women on institutional board.
North Carolina	No	NA	NA	NA	Yes	$10	Yes	Through social workers	
Ohio	No	No	Yes	Civil Service	Yes	$50	1	Parole officer and others	
Oregon	Newly established as separate institution; no policies or procedures available								
Pennsylvania	No	No	Yes	Political appointment	Home furlough*	$10	**	Parole officer and others	*May be for work or for other reasons **Beginning halfway house
Rhode Island	Women's Reformatory closed. Information received Oct. 30, 1972								
South Carolina	No	No	NA	NA	Yes	Bus fare	Yes	Assistance given; kind of help varies.	
Texas	No	No	NA	NA	Yes	$5 + bus fare	Yes	Vocational rehabilitation, Texas Employment Committee	
Tennessee	No	1	2	Political appointment	Yes	Yes; no am't stated	Yes	Parole officers, counselors*	*Seven Step Program
Virginia	No	No	Yes	Political appointment	Yes	$20	No	Vocational rehabilitation pre-release counseling, employment commission	
West Virginia	No	No	No	NA	No	$5	No	Parole officers	
Wisconsin	No	No	No	Civil Service	Yes	$10	Yes	Vocational rehabilitation	
Washington	No	1	1 black	Not political	Yes*	$40**	No	Vocational rehabilitation, public assistance and others	*May be for job or job training **Several 'gate money' options. Clothing and transportation given

Key: NA—no answer given
*—see Other Information column

Parole Preparation—Summary

Only three states appear to have a separate board to hear women's cases. Fifteen report that their parole boards are made up of members appointed by the governor, commissioner or other political official. Such appointees may or may not be prepared for such duties. Colorado, Ohio, and Wisconsin make appointments from a Civil Service list. Two say that appointments are not political but give no basis for selection of board members. Ten states did not answer the question.

Seventeen states have at least one minority member on the parole board.

Twenty-five states are using some kind of work release or work furlough program. Although there have been "walk-aways" (escapes) among the women while on the program, both staff and residents feel this is one of the most rehabilitative programs in operation.

The halfway house plan is also growing in popular use. Nineteen states already have this kind of help for the newly paroled person, while two others are planning one or more. These vary in policy of operation from the tightly regulated to the loosely structured.

Among the very new halfway houses, PREP House in Sacramento is an excellent example of positive operation. In its eighteen months of existence, 153 women have gone through the house. There have been only four cases of parole violation so serious that the woman was returned to an incarcerated status.

Aside from halfway house help when available, the states give other and different kinds of assistance. Some are doing a great deal to help a woman cope with the very serious problems sure to arise during her first weeks outside. Parole officers, community volunteers, churches, vocational rehabilitation programs, Trade Advisory Committees and others, programs to help women with drug or alcohol problems are all helpful.

One of the great weaknesses which appears to be present in all states reporting is the small amount of money given upon release to help a woman support herself until her first paycheck. Release money ranges from zero to $100. Even $100 is not a realistic sum to live on for at least two weeks, more likely a month or more. The few who have had jobs for small wages in prison may have saved a little, but this will be the exception rather than the rule.

A limited number have income sources outside— a husband, parents or friends—but prison inmates are not generally wealthy, nor do they come from wealthy families who are both willing and able to help. Too often a parolee's family members not only cannot help but are even embarrassed to have her return to them.

The entire area of parole preparation needs the support of an informed public.

BIBLIOGRAPHY

American Correctional Association. *Correctional Institutions and Agencies of America, Canada and Great Britain.* Maryland: 1970.

Bennett, James V. *I Chose Prison.* New York: 1970.

California Department of Corrections, Research Division. *California Prisoners.* Sacramento: 1968.

California Department of Justice, Bureau of Criminal Statistics. *Crime and Delinquency in California.* Sacramento: 1969.

Carter, Iverne R. "Correctional Programs for the Woman Offender." Paper given at Governor Brown's Conference on Crime and Delinquency, May 20, 1965. Mimeographed.

Clarion, August–December 1970, January 1971. CIW inmate newspaper.

Joint Commission on Correctional Manpower and Training. *Research in Correctional Rehabilitation.* Washington, D.C.: 1967.

—— *Targets for In-Service Training.* Washington, D.C.: 1967.

Sands, Bill. *My Shadow Ran Fast.* Englewood Cliffs, N.J.: 1964.

Sands, Bill. *The Seventh Step.* New York: 1967.

Scudder, Kenyon J. *Prisoners Are People.* Garden City, N.Y.: 1952.

Ward, David A. and Kassebaum, Gene G. *Women's Prison: Sex and Social Structure.* Chicago: 1965.

Zalba, Serapio R. *Women Prisoners and Their Families.* California Department of Social Welfare, Department of Corrections: 1964.